ATHEISTS' COMMON ERRORS

Eric Bright

Bright Press™

2018

Acknowledgements:
The typefaces used for the body of the text are from Linux Liberation G, Linux Libertine, and Linux Biolinum G families. The main typeface used in the title and back-cover is called Cardo, designed by David Perry. The other typeface used to create the glitched "error" word is called Hacked and is designed by David Libeau. The book is entirely typeset in LibreOffice. Bibliography is managed and created by a software called Zotero. The cover is designed in Adobe Illustrator. The human/DNA element of the cover-design is created by Freepik and its DNA Codis element in the background is created by Vecteezy.com. All of these names and trademarks belong to their respective owners.

Copyright © 2018 by Eric Bright

All rights reserved.

Published by BRIGHT PRESS™. BRIGHT PRESS™ is a trademark of Eric Bright Publisher.

First edition released in: April 2018
Version 1.0.0
ISBN-13: 978-0 993 786 013
ISBN-10: 0 993 786 014

www.brightpress.ca

Table of Contents

Introduction..6

PART ONE

When things go wrong..................................10

    Losing faith...10

    Social issues..11

    What is next? Misery!.............................13

    Propaganda against disbelief................16

    What are the benefits?..........................19

    Too many questions..............................21

    So much knowledge..............................23

    Biology...28

    The atheist literature............................32

    The attitude..34

    Why is it impossible?............................38

    There is a problem in here...................42

    What can be bashed, what cannot........44

    Disparity! A big one!.............................46

    No obligation..56

    Atheists are happy................................59

    Denial...62

- The measure of success............63
- A taste of your own medicine............65
- The cost of lost opportunities............67
- Jerry DeWitt style............69

Writing about atheism with religious minds in mind 71

- Denial............72
- Cognitive dissonance............75
- Inclusion, control, affection............77
- Universal love............81
- Rush............84
- Emotional interference............86
- Social rejection & emotional pain............88
- Alternatives............92
- Emotional needs............97
- Constructed False Memory............102
- Confirmation bias............106
- Good intention............112
- Christmas Bundle: Buy 1, get 4 free............118
  - Loss and grief............118
  - Hope............120
  - Meaning............125

Fear..134

Self-deception..................................139

Mystified..154

Self-initiated change........................156

Part Two

What to do and what not to do................162

Selective Atheism.............................162

As nonbeliever as you.......................162

They know all about you...................164

Emotions..169

"Playing Chess with a Pigeon"..........170

Define the defeating conditions.......172

Define the terms...............................173

Everyone is a selective atheist..........177

You explained it; so what?................179

Incentives...182

Flooding a debate.............................187

Changed their mind? Nope!..............191

All we can do..196

In a glance.......................................197

Bibliography...198

Introduction

The purpose of this book is to discuss all the ways atheists fail in debates and to suggest a few solutions to several common errors in atheists' arguments and argumentations.

This book is divided into two parts.

In part one I bring up tens of different ways that atheists lose their audiences in debates. Understanding the many typical types of mistakes that atheists make when they engage in most conversations with believers would be crucial in order to find better ways to deal with them. Unless we know our weak points in our conversations or debates, we would not be able to fix them.

It is a shame that only a few instances out of thousands of similar short or long conversations between theists and atheists ever bear any fruit. If you are an atheist and you wonder how is this possible, then part one of this book is for you. It demonstrates, via many examples, how most of our dialogues with theists fail.

Also, part one tells you where believers come from, what is in the back of their minds before, during, and after a conversation, and what sort of backgrounds make them who they are, and behave the way they do. Unless you can genuinely sympathize with those you try to have a constructive conversation with, you will not be able to engage them in a useful conversation. Your dialogue will eventually become something like, "I said blah blah, and they said blah blah." Before you can even hope to make them see the world from a fresh perspective, you need to know why most believers deserve a lot better than what atheists are ready to grant them in most dialogues. Only then can your approach and your communication tone becomes respectful enough so your audience might start hearing you.

Part two of the book deals with the question of why most theist-atheist dialogues fail and what we might be able to do about them.

There are times that you can avoid wasting everyone's time in a debate as well as your passive but watchful audience. Also, you will notice that there are types of debates that are doomed to fail no matter what.

In general, as a good debater, and particularly as a good atheist debater, you might want to learn ways to determine the message you want to convey, why your approach might not be working, and what else you might be able to do to be more clear, more effective, and less wasteful in conversations you will have with believers.

Believe it or not, many atheists, even some famous ones, don't actually know what it means to be an "atheist" and what the term actually entails. Some think that "atheism" is an idea or a set of ideas to be defended. Many believe that atheism is a belief in itself. As such, many debaters try to defend "it." Quite a lot of problems can easily be avoided just by clarifying what it is to be an "atheist" and what the term means. This, too, is one of the objectives of the second part of this book.

Once you finished reading this book, you will be able to have a broad perspective on the issues and challenges that most, if not all, atheist debaters face when they try to discuss anything with most believers.

Hopefully, you will gain a new appreciation and respect towards many believers whom you might try to engage in a conversation in the future.

You will be informed on most of the ways that you can be seen as arrogant, ignorant, intolerant, untactful, callous, or plain insensitive. You will also learn why these perceptions of you might form in the minds of your audience and how, if at all, to fix them.

At the end, you will learn why you ought to respect your interlocutors, when to engage in a conversation, and when to avoid them, what pitfalls to watch for, and strategies to, stick to in order to become a better debater and communicator.

Now, let's start our journey from a place you might be familiar with before we jump into the rabbit hole. You, or someone you know, might have lost their faith at some point. Let's start there.

PART ONE

When things go wrong

"Don't speak unless you can improve on the silence."[1,2]

Losing faith

Let us assume that a person with an honest intent and no, or very little, self-deception wants to figure out the legitimacy of his faith. Whatever his faith might be, there are thousands of ways to approach this task. Some of these ways are guaranteed to cause a reverse effect that is to say not only they will not inform and enlighten him, but also they will make him a more faithful person.

That is not good. I would even say that it is disastrous. How can one find the shortest and the most accurate way to learn about the reality of a religious faith? Is there even such a path available?

At the first glance, the landscape might look overwhelming. Our honest man or woman might find himself in a library of ideas, some opposing others. If he already knew what the truth was, he would not have needed any guidance. He would have known the truth and no journey would have been needed. But, the problem is that he does not know what the truth is and that is why he has started to question his faith in the first place.

How can he tell a propaganda apart from an honest attempt to understand the world and to seek truth? The solution seems to be complicated to our friend. Specially if he does not have the right tools, or ingredients so to speak, to sound thinking. That is right. Our thinking can very easily be in error, and very often so. Error in our reasoning and arguments are the main reasons why this whole game of religion faiths has started at all. Had we been good thinkers, we would not have made so many obvious mistakes in our world-views, and we would have corrected them once we caught the errors.

Faulty reasoning is only one of the reasons why religions started. There are social, political, and even financial reason to the creation of religions. But, for whatever reason a religion is created, faulty reasoning is a *must*, to keep it going. This is usually accompanied by lack of knowledge, misinformation, wishful thinking, and organized systems that directly benefit from this mixture of elements (such as churches).

What if our honest man has already sensed that something fishy is going on, and he wants to figure it out? He wants to get to the bottom of the issue if possible. How should he proceed?

Social issues

Being who we are and where in the fabric of a society we are embedded, it is a challenge to shake things up. Our families and friends might be looking up to us. They might have many expectations from us. They might want us to join them in church services that they attend. To be living amongst a group of church-goers creates a very complicated situation for those who want to question their faith. It makes the task look almost impossible.

The stakes are too high. Our friend does not only want to ask questions about his own thoughts and beliefs, but also he will end up calling into question the validity of the beliefs of his family members, his friends, and almost everyone else he comes in contact with. This might not only become an embarrassing task with embarrassing results, but also it could be looked at as betrayal, backstabbing, or mean accusations. The prospect of such a move does not and cannot look all right. How could it?

What are you willing to sacrifice to get your hands on truth? How much is truth worth? Is it worth making one thousand and one enemies out of our beloved family members and friends? Is it worth losing our friends or breaking up relationships? How much are you willing to pay to learn the truth about, let's say, the origin of life? These questions and tens of similar ones show the high cost of any move such as the one our honest man is about to make. This is a serious matter. There might even be no return. Once a relationship breaks up, it might never reconnect, ever again. There is no guarantee that the people who know us today and who respect us today would do the say tomorrow when they discover that we have lost our faith.

That is scary. Who is ready to take that 'leap of faith' to lose faith? Who might be willing to rock the boat? With such a grim perspective in sight, we should not wonder why most faithful fellows seem to be unwilling to participate in a possible destruction of their own social lives. Why should they?

In some societies, he who abandons his faith must be killed, period.

What is next? Misery!

The problem is even more complex than that. Once our honest man starts questioning his beliefs, he might very well end up in a state of bafflement and perplexity. He might not know how to answer the questions he used to answer before with the help of the doctrines of his religion. This is every bit as serious a problem as the social issues surrounding the loss of faith itself. Who would then be the authority to tell him right from wrong? Where is he now supposed to get the assurances that his church used to give him?

Imagine that one day you "know" the purpose of life, you "know" why humans are here on earth, you "know" what will happen when you die, you "know" that you will see your beloved, deceased family members and friends. Imagine that you have clear answers for all of them and you feel safe and secure because of those answers. Imagine that "knowing" that you will see your beloved mother in the afterlife warms your heart and calms your anxiety. Imagine that "knowing" that someone is watching you and will compensate you for every wrongdoing that is done to you and will avenge, on your behalf, the injustices that has been done to you. How nice would that be?

Imagine that each time you have an exam, you "know" that there is someone who would take care of you even if you have not studied well during the semester. Imagine that you "know" that even if you fail your courses, that is because someone has a plan for you and things will eventually turn to your benefit.

Imagine that you are sick with pneumonia, have very painful cough that don't seem to ever end, your body aches badly, your head feels like it is going to explode, and you just wish you could die right now, right there. Imagine that you never mind any of that really, because you "knew" that everything was going to be perfectly fine, you would enter another realm, you would see the departed, the friends who have passed away years ago, your ancestors, and everyone else you ever wanted to reunite with. Imagine that you "knew" that the ones you were going to leave behind were going to be taken care of by the hands of the most benevolent being. How cool is that?

Now that you imagined all of those, let us turn the table and see what will happen if you lose faith.

To being, let us assume that you wake up one day and, as if by magic, you find yourself not being able to believe in anything you used to believe in until yesterday. You can suddenly see that what you used to believe, that is all of the above, were all false beliefs. They were either wishful thinking or illusions.

According to your new perspective, you clearly recognize that you did not actually "know" any of those things. You did not "know" if you would enter another realm, would see the departed and everyone else you ever wanted to reunite with. You did not "know" that the ones you were going to leave behind were going to be magically taken care of by the hands of the most benevolent being. You did not even know if such a being exists.

In that case, you realize that any wrong that is done to you can very easily go unpunished. All the injustice that you have been put through can easily be forgotten. Not only that, they might even easily go unnoticed. You would see all the wishes you ever had and all the unfulfilled hopes of yours might easily remain unfulfilled. That is not all. You will realize that there will be no afterlife at all, and all that you have, and all what you ever had is this very life, which is gone anyway.

You see it clear that when you are in trouble, there will not be an invisible hand, pulling you out of it, and when you have an exam, there will not be anyone with a special plan just for you to make you pass the test. When you fail, you will not be compensated for it in any other life. You are as insignificant as any other living organism on this planet, on the same plane as a worm or a bacterium. You are not special at all. A tree and a fish have as much importance as you have. And worse than all of these, you are alone when you are alone. There is no one else there but you and the conversation you have with yourself is in your head.

Now, how cool is that? Not cool at all! Who wants it? Screw that!

The question is that who in his right mind would ever want to feel like that? That feels like crap, doesn't it? I bet it would if you do not know what to do with yourself when you are alone.

Not a small complication, I bet. A prospect such as this is certainly not anything that anyone would ever look forward to embracing. After all, why should anyone embrace such a cold perspective when the alternative is a cosy and warm feeling filled with hope, anticipations, and welcoming prospects?

At least, the people of faith are told that such is the deal they are going to get if they question their faith or abandon their religions, which takes us to the next issue.

Propaganda against disbelief

The people of faith are told that the religion you are in is love, beauty, transcendental feelings, spirituality, warmth, hope, future, justice, and all the goodies that are promised in the book. The alternative, they are told, is cold, rigid, inhumane, hopeless, void of love, filled with emptiness (!), lack of beauty, trivial, purposeless, dead, and all the ugly things you can imagine. One side of the deal is all good and the other side of the deal is all evil.

The people of faith are told these things at every chance the stewards of their faiths have to tell them anything. If you want love, you can only find it in your own religion (and all the rest of the thousands of other religions are "of course" wrong and mislead).

The people of faith are warned, at every opportunity, that leaving their faith would certainly and irrevocably break everything in their lives. Not only that, but also it will bring the wrath of the invisible forces upon those who dare abandon their faith.

Again, the stakes are very high. You either stay where you are, and then are welcomed into the kingdom of heaven or wherever else your faith proposes to you as the ultimate good place for your soul to dwell at, or you will be doomed in the most horrible way that the imagination of the priests could conjure up. You either live forever in the spirit, the good, and achieve nirvana, or you will be sent to the lowest of the lows to burn in the most fierce fires for eternity or be reincarnated into lower animals and keep experiencing an almost never-ending suffering and misery.

This would sound like a big deal to anyone who has never come across any other deal before. It might even sound plausible to a simple mind. Even smarter minds can be made scared of this crap. Who would like to be handed such a horrible deal after all?

The protectors of faith go into extreme lengths to picture "the" hell to the followers of their faith as fearsome as possible. They won't stop at anything to depict "the" consequences of even the slightest acts of rebellion. They want to be heard loud and clear. They even believe in what they say. Many of them sincerely and deeply believe in what they will tell you about the miseries that will fall upon anyone who refuses to follow their orders.

What would you do if you think that you "know" what horrible fate is awaiting your poor fellow human beings and you can avert it by pulling them onto the right track? Would you stay aside and watch them burn? Would you take it easy and let them find the right way by trial and error while you already "know" what the right way is? I bet you won't do any of these. You won't dare standing aside with your hands crossed watching your fellow human beings turn into ashes. Who would do such a horrible thing anyway?

Or that is what you would firmly believe if you think that you "know" the right way from the wrong.

Do we have to be a rocket scientist to see what can be gained by adhering to the teachings of your faith and encouraging others to enter it too? Facilitating, so to speak, the transition from the realm of evil to the kingdom of god? If that is what it amounts to?

If our honest man is the one who wants to step into a path with so many perceived dangers as I mentioned above, then it is easy to see why he would be totally reluctant to even take the first step; to even considering that possibility. Wouldn't it be frightening to get into such a gamble? Not everyone enjoys gambling after all, right? Most people around him are probably going to stay where they are and be saved as he is told. He will be left alone to face his own demise. This is what he has been warned about all the way from the moment he learned to talk; almost. He would sincerely believe that if he steps outside of his comfortable zone, he will hand over his eternal bliss to the devil and will be handed over an eternal damnation and suffering. He is told that all odds are going to be against such a stupid move. If the premises are true, as everyone around him has been telling him they are, then such a move would justifiably be called stupid, wouldn't it?

He is presented with a dilemma since he can remember: Either go to heaven or go to hell.

What are the benefits?

"Nothing," he is told repeatedly. There won't be anything in losing his faith. Nothing whatsoever. There will only be destruction, damnation, misery, and demise. Nothing will be gained by disbelieving in the doctrine of his religion and everything will be lost.

What benefits really? Most likely, he cannot even mention one, a single one. Even if he tries, he won't be able to come up with only one genuine advantage that a life without faith in his religion might have over his own life. Isn't it interesting? Not even one!

What would you have done had your pastor told you that quantum mechanics has already shown that disbelief is futile (never mind the proof)? What would you have done had your pastor told you that the god particle is discovered by physics and is a testament to the validity of the church and good faith? Maybe you haven't heard it directly from your pastor's mouth, but you might know someone who has heard him saying just those things; loud and clear. Wouldn't it be totally pointless to go against the tide and deny such clear evidence of the validity of your religion? It would be insane to do so if all the evidence is pointing to one "fact": That Jesus Christ, the living god, is vindicated. When physics discovered the "god" particle, who are you to say otherwise?

Would it be beneficial to go against the reality of physics and quantum mechanics to deny the truth of your faith? No one would think so.

As you can see, the faithful will not be able to see any advantage in taking a step against his religious beliefs. The society is literally saturated by the stories of how horrible faithlessness is and how hopeless, miserable, pathetic, and evil disbelievers are. No one seems to have ever heard anyone talking about the benefits of such a lonely, low life anyway. If he has not heard anything in that regard yet, then there shouldn't be any. He, religiously, browses his Facebook feeds every day and, in virtue of that, he thinks that he is fully informed of things that happen in the world. How could any benefit of disbelief be discovered, right under his nose, without him even noticing it? He thinks that it is impossible.

Not only that, but also he has read William Lane Craig's book called *Reasonable Faith* and in there he is convinced that his faith is reasonable. Also, he has read several books on why *The God Delusion* has got it totally wrong. He has visited the Creationist museum and everything in there was pointing to one thing and one thing only: That god, not just any god but the biblical god, has created this world with him in mind. He cannot imagine why all of this can be wrong. What is possibly good about going against all of these "evidence" and denying the "truth" of his religion? If he cannot see anything good in such a rotten misstep, and if no one he read nor any "museum" he visited suggest that losing faith might be a good thing, even a bit, then why should he do otherwise? Why should he lose his faith?

Too many questions

These questions and many others are quite serious concerns of those who honestly believe in the validity of their faiths.

Our honest man believes that he has never come across a single person who could properly answer any of those questions at all. He also believes that those questions cannot be answered in any different way than what he is taught in his faith. He is taught that any other answer rather than what he is given by the protectors of his faith are automatically invalid. Therefore, he sees no reason why he even needs to listen to any of them anyway.

That is why he has never listened to anyone who tried to convince him to the contrary. They were wrong anyway, and he "knew" it already. So, he is saving everyone's time and energy and doing others a great service by not listening to any disbeliever or to anyone who wants to question anything about his religion. This way, he thinks, he is doing them good. He might even think that by not listening to those evil voices, the voices of a cold and miserable void, he does two good deeds instead of one: On the one hand he is not allowing those lost souls to commit yet another sin, and on the other hand he is not letting himself to go astray. Hitting two birds with one stone.

If his pastor says that disbelievers are misled, if W. Craig says that his faith are on strong footings, if the creationist museum demonstrates that the Bible is an accurate historical account of what really happened at the moment of creation, there should be absolutely no doubt that he must stick to his gun and remain faithful. His grandparents had always been members of the same congregation as his, and they surely would have come to the same conclusion.

His mother used to tell her all the time that this is the correct faith and this is the right way to live. He studied "many other" religions (which ironically ended up being a total of two: Protestantism, Catholicism) and figured out that all the world religions say almost the same things with some slight variations. That is why he strongly feels that he knows everything there is to be known about all religions. He has heard about Islam and Judaism, but he is told that they don't really matter because they all are either wrong or worship false idles. So, they don't even count. Even if they count, by any stretch of his imagination, then he is told that they are both distorted copies of Christianity; even Judaism? "Of course," he is told.

So much knowledge

He believes that he has studied all religions deep enough to know that either all of them are wrong, or they are saying exactly the same thing that his own religion says; only the labels might be different.

So much knowledge! Wow! By this time, he "knows" that all biology is a fabrication and a slide of hands. That evolution is certainly false and even impossible. That the Biblical account of creation is definitely the only way anyone can ever explain anything about this world. That all creation accounts in thousands of other religions, even with way more followers than his own religion, are wrong. That the three or five books he has read (including the Bible, the William's books, and Harry Potter) tell him the truth while all other books are merely a bunch of bullshit put together by ill-informed disbelievers to mislead him at best. That he will go to heaven while everyone else will not (unless they believe in exactly the same things that he believes in), and many other things. These and a few other "facts" make up the body of his "knowledge."

With so much knowledge (he thinks it is a lot anyway), he reserves the right to believe that he is right and everyone else who does not think the same way is wrong. How could it be otherwise if he possesses the truth and others don't? They would eventually end up being misled.

I don't mean it pejoratively. He thinks that he knows quite a lot about the world. He also counts his life experience as a big part of his knowledge (the Harry Potter books too).

Everyone thinks that they are special, that they are different from others, that they have something in their essence that makes them so unique that they deserve a medal or something for that uniqueness. Maybe not a medal in reality, but some serious recognition. So, everyone deeply believes that they have seen all there is to be seen, that they have gained just enough insight into the way the world is spinning that makes them significantly different from the next person beside them.

This sense of uniqueness is something that most humans feel, even if secretly so. Even if they think that everyone else is pretty good, they also believe that they are just slightly better in some ways, they somehow know slightly more. Because they know slightly more than the person next to them and practically everyone else on this planet, then they are justified in believing what hey believe. A belief is true, in this case, in virtue of being *their* belief!

What they call 'their knowledge' is a mixture of all of these. And of course some stuff they vaguely remember from grade six, eleven, and other grades that they cannot pinpoint right now, but it will come to them later if they try to remember them hard enough.

While this is all good, they would not ever suspect that what they call knowledge might not actually tell them much, and most of it is either totally false or with so many holes that they won't count as knowledge by anyone's standard. Most people would never freely admit that.

This little extra insight that he thinks he has, makes all the differences to him. He believes that this extra insight is so unique that gives him all he needs to unlock the secrets of the universe, or at least what matters to him. He thinks that although there might be smart people on earth and some of them might even be quite smarter than himself, what he has gained is so special, so personal, and so his, that he doubt if it can be repeated by anyone else or be understood by anyone else. It is *his* knowledge after all. How can anyone else know it?

In many cases, he thinks that he has experienced certain things, so special, that he is a changed person because of that. Certain experiences that his mind cannot explain in any other way (or doesn't want to). To him, those experiences have proven the validity of his faith. He doesn't care that everyone else in all other religions also say the same thing and it would be impossible for all of them are true. Most religions believe in things that are opposite or contrary to the beliefs in other religions and there is no way that all of them can be true at the same time, but he does not care.

It does not make him feel weird if everyone else also firmly believes that it is his religion and *only* his religion that is true, and they also have their own "experiences" to support their claims. He never asks how it could be so. How could all of these opposing experiences all be true? Are they all true or not? Which creation story is the true story? All of them are different stories. They say completely different things, and they explain completely different events. All of them cannot be true at the same time. But, how come everyone adamantly believes in his version of the creation story as "the" true story? Why do they also claim that they have life experiences that "proves" the legitimacy of *their* version of the creation story? Something has to give, but they don't care about it even if they are lucky enough to notice the discrepancies.

When he talks to unbelievers, he already "knows" that those lost souls have not had the chance to experience what he has experienced or else they would not have been lost souls to begin with. Only if they "knew" what he knows. Only if they had the same experiences as he had! Alas! He thinks that his knowledge is indisputable.

Usually when you corner him to tell you his unique and profound experiences, you will be given the accounts of a handful events (usually two or three) that has changed him so deeply. When you ask him if he had thought of any alternative explanations or even if he remembers the event as it actually happened rather than the way he wished it to happen, you will get the same answers without any exception. That his explanation is "the" only viable explanation for the event, even if he admits that other explanations might be possible too, and he remembers the event exactly as it happened. Exactly!

Although both of these answers are almost always wrong, he does not care. It has been shown conclusively that humans' memory is one of the least reliable forms of memories we can base our evidences on,[3–5] and there are almost always more than one alternative explanations for any given event, he doesn't care. For all it is worth, he might be making it all up. Every single bit of it, without him even knowing that he is making it up. He might very easily swapped the order of the sequence of events and now he remembers it in the order that confirms his convictions rather than the order that the real even actually took place. And for all what it is worth, the explanation that he is so stubbornly defending is usually the only explanation, amongst many others, with the lowest degree of possibility rather than the highest. If you mention these to him, although it might be very interesting and all, but he does not care after all, because he "knows" that he is right and you are wrong.

Biology

I suspect this is one of the most fundamental issues regarding the lack of motivation in most people to question their faiths. Let me explain.

It has been demonstrated that our evolutionary history has primed us to have the kind of predispositions that we carry around in our heads. Simply put, our biology is partially responsible for the emergence of supernatural thinking in our species, which in turn helped the emergence of religions. All of our discoveries in neuroscience point to this fact.[6-9]

A human brain is very similar to a universal machine in the sense that Alan Turing described such a machine. Because of that, it is capable of doing incredible things as well as incredibly stupid things. There is nothing in our biology that disallows us from doing moronic thing and thinking moronic thoughts. It is because when human brain is capable of doing more complex tasks, it would also be capable of performing less complex tasks too by default.

This capability is not necessarily a bad thing, unless when it is. When is it a bad thing then? The idea is that it would be bad if a capable machine instead of being used to its full potentials, is used to generate crappy results. It would be wasteful to say the least. It can even get worse. The same machine can be used to damage or destroy other machines. This is plain stupid. But despite its moronic qualities, the human brain is not in many great ways. To add insult to the injury, we can even see that this wonderful machine is actually used for destructive purposes in huge scales. Wars and all the things that are related to them are good examples for that.

Had it been the full extent to which human stupidity could go, we would have only a few serious issues like most other living organisms who fight to access better a territory, a better mate, more food, and such. But this is not it. Our biology compels us to fight over resources all right. But, it also contains the seeds to other forms of potential issues such as imagination.

Imagination is the source of our advancements in the past several thousand years. How fantastic is that! However, for the most part of our evolutionary history, this 'imagination' served us with 'images' that were not true in any sense *and* were not useful but hurtful. If our imagination was bound to make us happier and a lot less miserable, it would have been ideal. But this is not the case. Our imagination is not bound by too many things. That can eventually lead us to imagine things that do not exist. Nothing bad in that yet, right? I guessed so. But what if it pushes the envelope further and further? What if it generates more and more imaginary friends and compels us to believe in their existence? What if it becomes so powerful in its capability to 'imagine' that it becomes harder and harder to discover what it is 'imagining' is actually real or mere images?

That is what have happened to our species. If you live with those images in your head long enough, they appear quite real to you. This ability, i.e. to imagine things that do not exist, is not unique to humans. I can tell from my personal experience with my cat that he also sees things that are not there.

Here is what happens. Around a particular time in the evenings, he suddenly becomes alert. As if he is chasing a butterfly, he focuses on a point in the empty space in front of him and jumps towards it as if he is jumping on a prey. Then he makes a funny noise and runs away galloping. Then he suddenly freezes somewhere in the room, gazing into the empty space, and repeats his attack (or whatever he thinks he is doing). He keeps doing this for about a quarter of an hour until he gets tired of running around and chasing his imaginary prey.

Whatever he thinks he is chasing and whatever goes through his mind, it is obvious that there *is* something going on in his mind as if he is chasing after something. Even if he is not chasing after anything in his mind according to cats' culture, he is doing something. To bystanders such as humans, he looks like playing. He seems as if he is chasing after something that is not there, either to entertain himself or in a compulsory and involuntary way. That does not matter either. What matters is that it happens and it is a direct result of what is going through his brain, involuntarily or not. As for *what* is going through his brain or his mind if you wish, we might not be able to know it any time soon. But we know this much that something is going through his mind that compels him to do what he does when there is no good reason to do it at all. He won't catch any food, and for all purposes, he doesn't seem to get more fit than when he does not do it.

If we go so far to grant him the ability to entertain himself, it would follow that he is playing with something in his mind. Or maybe, something in his mind is playing a trick on him. Either way, he is responding to something—most likely in his mind—that is not part of the physical reality (except for it being the results of the physical reality of his brain and body).

My point is that it seems very reasonable to assume (unless the otherwise is demonstrated) that other animals too are able to imagine things. And not only that, but also those imaginations can become so strong and so vivid to them that they can make them act upon those imagined entities.

If the brains of animals seem capable of pulling off that trick on them, so can human brains. And here is where all the trouble begin.

The atheist literature

I have already explained it in my book *Religovirology* that why it seems to be highly unlikely, almost impossible, to change someone's faith if he is not already looking forward to seeing some changes. So, I won't repeat myself in here. Given the amount of pressure and the type of resistances that go against any such move to drop one's convictions, it should not surprise us why such a move usually does not occur.

Losing faith does not happen with the help of atheism, with what atheists write, with what they say, with their arguments, with their efforts, or with their books. Those who will end up giving up the faith in their religions would do it anyway, with or without atheists' help, and those who are destined not to change it, usually will not. This, of course, is decided not based on looking at someone's horoscope, but by his predispositions.

In other words, some types of personalities are a lot more vulnerable than other types to be sucked into a web of dreams and never get out. Nevertheless, distinguishing the vulnerable type from the immune type might seem to be only possible in retrospect at first. Without having a large set of data to discover relationships and correlations, it would be hard to find such correlations just by looking at a group of people.

But even without having such a data set to study, we might still be able to see some signs. For example, even without looking at data, we can predict that a stressful life is more conducive to the generation or the maintenance of a more religious outlook than it is to an atheistic one.[10,11] And guess how many people have plenty of stress in their lives! Or, without looking at data, we can already predict that being raised in a religious family does have a strong causal effect on the world-view of the children who live in the family, and the correlation is clearly positive. We also can predict that the other way around is not necessarily the case. That is, being raised in an atheist family does not have a strong effect on a child to make him an atheist (for several reasons. One is that atheist parents usually don't force their world-view down their children's throats. And children are a lot more likely to be constantly bombarded by religious material and propaganda everywhere they go and every day, than being exposed to explicit atheistic material, and so on).

Atheists and the materials they produce are not going to help those who need it the most. Those materials will be picked up by those who already have doubts and by those who already dare to ask questions. They would find their ways, albeit through a rougher or a longer path, by themselves anyway. A questioning mind who knows how to ask relevant questions will eventually reach the same conclusion that other similar minds have already reached. This is inevitable. But to those of us who might not even have doubts, not even knowing that we can question the pillars of our religions, or don't dare to do so, the atheist literature is almost useless.

I cannot think of a worse way to approach this matter than to hit it heads on. Not only does it not work, but also it will backfire. Sometimes very strongly so.[12] Not only that, but also we recently found that some of the humans' most cherished persuasion techniques actually backfire significantly more than it works.[13] For instance, presenting a religious person with tons of facts that directly challenge his faith would most likely do more harm than good. Maintaining a constant and strong eye contact does not do any better either. It has been proven that both of those techniques are actually the ones you should avoid if you want to hold the slightest chance in getting close to persuading anyone.[12,13]

And yet, those are almost invariably the ways that atheism is presented to the faithful. The failure of acceptance is almost guaranteed.

The attitude

The problem goes a few steps deeper. Do you remember the advice: "Don't be a dick!"? You should. It was not long ago when Phil Plait gave his talk with the same title to highlight one of the main problems when atheists try to persuade the faithful.[14-16] I have not come across many atheists who tried to be a dick when presenting their case to their fellow religious friends, but on the Internet, that is exactly the vibe you would get almost anywhere you go. For some reason, people are such jerks when it comes to arguing their cases; specially online.

To everyone's credit, most people become jerks on the Internet under the condition of anonymity. Go to any online forum and try to disagree with the zeitgeist of the place and see how you are greeted. Most of us become jerks when we feel safe in freely expressing our disagreements without the fear of serious repercussions or retributions. So, it is not only some atheists who turn into jerks when they try to argue their point of view with those who think otherwise. It is most of us.

However, regardless of it being done consciously or not and anonymously or not, being a dick won't help to advance our cause.

> "In some specific places, the tone of what we are doing is decaying. [...] Let me ask you a question here. How many of you here today used to believe in something, "used to," past tense, whether it was flying saucers, psychic powers, religion, anything like that? You can raise your hand [...]. Now let me ask you a second question. The second question is, how many of you no longer believe in those things, you became sceptic, because somebody got in your face screaming and called you an idiot, brain-damaged, and a retard? Okay? Yeah! Right!"[14]

I need to be very hard-pressed to think that a poor communication technique can win the day. It might win in some cases. We already know that. For example, we know that "ridicule, insult, [and] gentle reminder" would actually work in some simple cases.[17] But we also know that it usually and immediately causes "counter-arguing, attitude bolstering, source derogation, and negative affect"—whatever that latter term means—which indeed works against persuasion efforts and cause strong resistance to persuasion.[18]

Ridicule triggers resistance to persuasion. Insult triggers resistance to persuasion. They work in limited cases for very simple and obvious issues that cannot be covered up in any sensible way, but religious matters are not obvious, they are not simple issues, and they can very easily be covered up in ways that can appear to make sense at the first glance.

Getting into arguments creates counterargument. Attitude bolstering causes attitude bolstering. Derogatory tones prompt derogatory tones. Ridicule and insult bring up all of the above at once.

Again, all the researches very clearly show what not to do and where not to go, and yet, there is where a lot of atheists go and that is what a lot of them do, as if they are in a fight club.

Maybe we feel defensive. Maybe we feel cornered. Maybe we feel oppressed and discriminated against. All of these feelings can make an air of distrust and animosity in us. We are all humans and our bodies and minds work almost the same ways. We are all animals and when we feel we are threatened, we jump into the fight-or-flight-or-freeze response, exactly like other mammals. In the heat of an argument, we can lose track of that effect and, confident of the truth being on our side, we might attack in such a brutal way that there *won't be any* counter-attack possible to be returned to us than responding in kind.

We can make it so difficult to sound agreeable that when we listen to ourselves saying the words that we have said, we might find it hard to agree with ourselves only because we sounded so angry.

Certainly not all atheists are like that, not all arguments are advanced with that attitude, and not all writers or speakers approach their audiences with such a bullish predisposition. There are tons of eloquently performed speeches, brilliantly written books, and gently argued conversations in the market generated by genius atheists. At the same time, there are also plenty of impulsive responses, immature and derogatory tones, and badly presented defences out there too. And guess what: A good way of destroying a position is to defend it poorly. Intentionally or not, it will generate the desired effect in the eyes of the opponent.

As we can see, some freethinkers actually damage the reputation and the acceptability of their own positions by simply defending it badly. By not being able to gain their ways into the hearts of their audiences, they make it even harder for others to inform the misinformed. Others who otherwise could have been received with open arms and ears, now might have a hell of a worse time in even finding someone who would lend them an ear.

In the light of this assessment, this group of defenders of truth are the most damaging offenders. As such, they would be doing enormously more good by simply shutting up and doing nothing.

There has been a recent study that demonstrates that: "When facts threaten their world-views, religious participants frame specific reasons for their beliefs in more unfalsifiable terms."[19] The reporter at ArsTechnica concluded that "[...] identifying why people resort to unfalsifiability, and avoiding making people defensive about their beliefs [...] could encourage people to let go of unfalsifiable beliefs."[20] This sounds easier to say than to do.

Why is it impossible?

Even if we have the strongest case in our hand, supported by unquestionable evidence and flawless and undeniable logic, corroborated by every single experiment that has ever been done and accurate to the tenth decimal point, observed by everyone, everywhere, at all time, reproducible by anyone who ever dare to reproduce it, and supported by all the rest of the knowledge that human beings have ever created, day in and day out, still we will fail to persuade a lot of people if we consider the compound effects of the combined elements that go against us. Our best shouts will fall on deaf ears if all odds are against us.

In this case, it certainly looks as if all odds are actually against us. There is a small chance that a previously-deeply-religious person changes suddenly and wakes up from his deep slumber by reading atheist literature, watching a documentary in that spirit, or attending a speech in that vain. It is possible. It really happens now and then. But, the bad news is that it gets harder and harder to persuade anyone of the truth of a very complex intellectual position if we start our conversations with the assumption that our audience is a bunch of morons, and let them know that too.

Even if they are a bunch of morons, I believe that the time and age has changed, and we all agree to have special schools for people with special needs and slow-pace learning abilities, right? What makes those "morons" any different from those people with special needs? Why are we treating the people with special needs with utmost respect and consideration while have almost zero tolerance towards our fellow religious friends who don't seem to get it? Yes, obviously they don't seem to get it. They might really have a hard time to wrap their minds around the ideas that we quickly comprehend. They might feel that their brains would explode if they think too hard while working on any equation that has anything more than a plus sign and an equal sign. There are people who genuinely feel terrible if they are demanded to think about complex matters. They feel a very uncomfortable tension in their bodies. Then they feel hot, or cold, then they feel that their brain is about to explode.

When are we going to accept that these people can also be respected the same way that we respect people with special needs?

It is also obvious that not all religious people are like that. There are many intelligent people who happened to be religious. The same way that there are many dumb atheists who don't instigate any sense in anyone but disgust and contempt. However, it is funny and unfair to still respect those dumb atheists, only because they are atheist after all, and look down on intelligent people who happened to believe in fairy tales of this or that brand of religion. If holding a double-standard is not good, it is not good for all.

The question is how do we react if we come across a moron atheist? Not a jerk atheist, but a moron one? We might try to gently and patiently explain things to him. We might think that he is slow in some way, and we might stop our efforts to teach him the subject in question. We might try different approaches. We might simply give up, accepting that he is not going to get it. But one thing would be clear. We won't call him names, and we won't look down on him. We might know, for a fact, that he is a moron atheist, because, let's say, he is in an atheist forum, tries to be polite and pleasant, expresses his atheism, and at the same time does not show any sign of intelligence at all. In our private thoughts we might decide that, patently, he is a moron. But I haven't seen, not often enough to be able to recall the incidence, that in such a forum, such a person being brutally attacked and verbally abused. Everyone would feel awful if they see such a thing happen.

But, Zeus forbid, if a fellow theist happens to be unfortunate enough to join that atheist forum. All hell will break loose. Please waste no time to show such a brutal face and greet him with sharpened-nails claws and fearsome teeth that the poor fellow would be burnt to ashes before he even realizes it. The question is: Is it possible to persuade anyone of anything under that condition?

Let's not be fools because the answer is an unambiguous "No!" As if such an obvious answer is actually very hard to comprehend, the current state of the affairs suggest that the dominant tone of the dialogues between the two parts of this divide is hostile to the extreme.

Being angry at the crimes religions have committed and keep committing against humanity is both justified and warranted.[21] It is alright to be angry with religions. It is alright, and is arguably necessary, to put religions down to their rightful graves where they belong. It is a fair game to bash religions with the hardest attacks that our species can muster. All of these are defensible.

But, in a conversation with another human being, none of those things can effectively turn anyone's mind away from any religion. If the purpose of a dialogue is to persuade, then those methods will always fail pathetically.

There is a problem in here

I am serious. We have a problem on our hands. On the one hand, what atheists say and complain about is justified. When they are asked to be gentle on other members of a forum, community, or gathering where atheists are in charge:

> "If it is something that pertains to their life and personal stories and how they came to see Chutluh as their lord and savior, save yourself the judgement and conversion speech and try to understand where they are coming from."

Then they complain that:

> "So we can now expect, and are forced to accept, the story of every trolling Christian/Muslim/other that wants to come in here and tell us about the 'love they feel' from some sort of skydaddy? We can't call a spade a spade when they talk about their 'evidence' and 'knowledge' of how all of this came to be?
>
> Isn't this supposed to be a safe-haven for atheists not a soap-box factory for theists? I'm confused by this [request]. I am angered by this

[request]. Perhaps it was just poorly worded, but it sure sounds like we now need to put up with whatever sort of nonsense a theist wants to spew in the name of 'understanding'."

No, we don't have to. Nobody has to.

But, I would argue that this complaint, although it is logical for different reasons, misses the mark completely and is a correct answer to the wrong question.

There are many differences between an idea, like a religion meme, and a person who holds that idea, like a religious person. These two are two completely different things and deserve two completely different approaches to be addressed.

As our species is getting smarter and more knowledgeable, it is imperative on every one to hold us accountable for what our collective understanding of the world is contaminated with, or can be contaminated with. We should not allow our wishful thinking get in our way of our clear comprehension of the world. We should guard the right, the ethical, the humane, the sustainable, the peaceful, and the logical way of thinking, living, and learning. We have a duty to disallow, reject, and debunk quackery, fraud, cheats, misinformation, organized crime, dogmatism, hatred, and bigotry. All citizens of the world have these duties. We have duties before ourselves, our planet, and every other object on earth, alive or inanimate, if we wish to ever see the dawn of our civilization. Even the slightest neglect, can cause devastating, long-term, and irreversible consequences. We have to have zero tolerance for pollution both in our physical and in our intellectual environments. All of these are respectable goals and ideals to adamantly seek. Those who are trying to bring about these ideals are admirable. We cannot question that.

Nevertheless, all of the above are different tasks from our other, equally important, social duties towards other human beings. If we want to uphold peace, we have to be peaceful. If we want to spread love and understanding, we have to love, be lovable, and understanding. If we want to teach others the differences between nonsensical fairy tale and reality, we have to be pleasant to ears, so we can be listened to so that we might teach. How can anyone teach anything to others by making himself as unlovable and unbearable as possible?

What can be bashed, what cannot

Ideas can be bashed as hard as possible. Bad ideas must be weeded out at all cost and mercilessly. Any system of belief that divides the societies and damages the integrity of humanity as a whole and all other organisms on this planet should be critically scrutinized, dismantled, and ideally be replaced by systems of thoughts that teaches harmony, peace, unity of life, love, trust, teamwork, foresights over short-sightedness, less greed, more sharing, freedom, democracy, and sustainability of systems over reckless expansions. All these are good and desirable. No society can afford tolerance towards war, division of its parts, constant fighting, poverty, greed, unchecked hunger for power, and unlimited wishful thinking. Otherwise, the history has shown repeatedly that societies start to rot from within and become easy prey to other unchecked powers ready to swallow them up and ruin all of their achievements. Or societies fall due to their unsustainable ways of life. Societies turn into hell because of the dominance of religious ideologies (e.g. crusades, the age of inquisitions, religious wars, etc.).

But, bashing ideas are different from bashing people who hold those ideas. Challenging ideas is not the same as challenging people. Ridiculing stupid ideologies and insulting stupid individuals are not the same.

It is one thing to find a book ridiculous and write about how stupid, misleading, misinformed, and absurd that book is, and it is another thing to tell someone that he is stupid because he is reading a ridiculous book.

It is one thing to publicize information on the damage and destruction that religions have been causing humans, and it is another thing to call someone the follower of a damaging and destructive religion.

All of those accusations are true, and truth won't change only because we are stuck in our humanly circumstances and are bound by our human limitations and sensitivities. But the same truths won't be accepted if the same sensitivities are bluntly ignored to present the truths.

In a typical conversation, it is a challenge to keep these two aspects separated. It needs a lot of debating skills and critical thinking not to mix up these two issues. And, sadly enough, this mixing up happens in the way atheism is argued as often and as awfully as it can be found in the arguments of theists. It seems that these two group of people sometimes share very similar traits: lack of etiquette and sympathy.

Disparity! A big one!

It is, however, mention-worthy that the faithful believers have been mastering the art of persuasion and converting others to their faiths for the past several thousand years. And they have become very good at it. They have learned when to talk, what to say, and how; when to avoid saying things, how not to irritate their audience, how to appeal to their audience's sense of awe, how to appeal to their emotions, how to appeal to their 'hearts', and how to pull them in.

If you have the most ridiculous idea in the world, an idea that any four-years child would immediately recognize as stupid, and then work on your techniques at persuading others to believe in that stupid idea for three thousand years, then what would you think your latest performance would result? Would you get a poor result or a good result, or a great result? I dare to say that the result of the experiment would go beyond being phenomenal.

Are you looking for an example of such an experiment? Search no more! Behold, millions of small and large religions around the world! Their successes at persuading people of the most absurd ideas and the most stupid, ridiculous, and even inhumane and cruel practices is indisputable. They have been putting up show after show of the most effective way of persuasion. Their skills are absolutely unparalleled in the world of atheism. Their methods are polished for thousands of years and cannot be challenged by any of the poorly administered ways that any atheist has ever tried to persuade anyone of anything.

It seems absurd that some atheist communities or individuals cannot, or have not yet, seen this enormous disparity of skills, powers, and tools. What can an atheist offer when a Christian appeals to his victim's insecurities, hopes, emotions, fears, desires, and heart? Absolutely nothing. Nothing that atheism uses, as its tools of persuasion, has anything to do with the way a faithful person can possibly be persuaded. Nothing atheism has in its arsenal of tools that matches, even remotely, the tools all fraudsters, magicians, pastors, priests, shamans, or the faith-healers have in their pockets.

There can be no doubt about these observations. The disparity between the skills are so vast that one wonders how to even begin to compare the two sides of this abyss. The reason is mainly because usually there is nothing comparable on the side of atheists and freethinkers that might have any hope of success.

What is wrong with the good works then? Here is what is wrong. Our writing style only speaks to atheists not to theists. It does not speak to our fellow believers because it does not speak their language. It does not connect with them because when it tries to, it uses the wrong words, the wrong tone, the wrong symbolisms, the wrong sentiments, the wrong emotions, the wrong stories, the wrong images, the wrong appeals, and the wrong mentalities. It can never pass its messages to its target audience because it does not encode it in the correct code that can be properly decoded by them, if it knows its target audience at all. It sounds as if it is taking to a bunch of like-minded fellows whereas nothing could be further from the truth than that.

Our best and most brilliant secular works are no match for poorest-worded speech that the least-literate priest ever delivered; if we mean it to be heard by the faithful that is. If we only wish to talk to ourselves, to regurgitate what we already know, to praise our own understanding of the world and tell ourselves how logical, how accurate, how realistic, and how sane we already are, by all means, we are free to do so. More power to those who want to do just that. But, that does not achieve the main objectives. That only reinforces our own convictions and positive feelings (not even our beliefs, because beliefs don't play a big role in the world of truth versus falsehood anyway).

If we are satisfied with telling our own jokes and being the only one who finds them funny, then good for us. But, then we shouldn't complain when no one even listens to us.

If we realistically look at what atheism have achieved so far, in terms of the power of persuasion, we would be disappointed. Because, basically, the atheism literature is written as if it is written for atheists by atheist. No attempt is made to actually speak to the heart of a truly-faithful religious reader. Except for a handful books and a handful talks that are written and given by very thoughtful authors here and there, the majority of the works that are out there is generally unsuitable for the purpose of persuading a believer. The methodology is wrong from A to Z. The language is immediately offensive in many cases. The attitude does not create an air of trust and well intention. The work is read by believers only to be criticised, not to be understood.

From the titles of the available books, to the way the contents are laid out, to the assumptions that the authors hold in their minds when they start their writings or speeches, to the sarcasm, and almost everything throughout their material is geared towards the wrong audience.

A group of mathematicians who are commissioned to write a first-grade textbook for a nation's schools throughout a country can, of course, start with the assumption that they are writing for a bunch of illiterate, virtually stupid, unskilled, attention defective, demonstrably incompetent in critical thinking, moronic brats. In some sense, those assumptions are not totally false either. Almost all first-graders are literally illiterate. They are all unskilled in countless number of things that really matter. Their brains are not fully developed which temporarily put them very close to the category of morons. They do lack attention, sometimes too horribly so. They are lacking most, if not all, tools of critical thinking. And last but not least, most of them are socially devilish and demonstrably underdeveloped in all manners of social conducts. These are those who mathematicians are actually writing for. But, imagine if they begin writing for them with those truths (they are not assumptions really) in mind. Start writing with those realities permeating through their words and leaking into their tones here and there. Giving the vibe that it is how the authors truly see their audiences. What do you expect to come out of it?

> "Even when the mouth lies, the way it looks still tells the truth."[22]
> — Nietzsche

In the example of the mathematicians, the assumptions of the authors are warranted and true. Now, when atheists write for themselves, they never carry such assumptions. Quite the opposite is true. The problem starts when they try to address their fellow religious human beings. Suddenly, as if they flipped a switch, all of those assumptions creep into their mentality and writing style. Any reader with the lowest level of reading competency can smell them from a mile away.

Do we want to be listened to or not? Do we want to make a difference or not? The current and all the future generations of people have enough atheistic literature to go through and learn how and why their doubts about their religions are warranted. There is no lack of guidelines, explanations, and eloquently-written scientific material that would easily enlighten anyone who has the slightest doubt in their mind about any religion. There is no problem, whatsoever, in that department. Truly, no extra material is needed. We have all what would take to guide anyone in doubt from the darkness of religion to the light of reality. These materials speak very well to the minds and the hearts of the already-doubtfuls.

But, boy! Let us see what we have in our libraries or book-stores to persuade those who do not have doubts in their minds about their beloved religion. If I don't call it a pathetic situation, I would call it an incredible triumph of absolute negligence.

No explanation, demonstration, speech, writing, or enlightening happens in isolation. People of faith who can read and write and come across an atheist's fellow-bashing speech or an atheist's demolishing, ridicule-ridden, *ad hominem* attack,[23] most probably have already read a bunch of other books and have listened to other speeches that have a lot better qualities, gentler, and more inviting. The battle of persuasion, if there can be any at all in this situation, is against a mountain of religious literature that is filled with hope (albeit unreal), love (albeit to bait the victims), welcome messages of brotherhood (to recruit members), appeal to emotions, tears, and miracle (to hook a poor soul in for eternity), scare techniques (to deter them from changing minds), promises on endless and unlimited happiness (to keep them in for enough time), cry for help (to fund churches and mosques and fill up their bank accounts), and tens of other fine-tuned and carefully crafted words and speeches.

People of faith read those words and listen to them, and by the time they encounter an atheist, they have already been soaked and saturated by those promises, hopes, fears, emotions, and sense of importance. They are told that they are important if they stay with this or that god or goddess. They are told that they will get goodies of all kind if they keep their ears and eyes shut. They are told that all of their problems will go away if they burn this or that sent in their houses, recite this or that prayer, and sacrifice a goat to the god of this or the saviour of that kind. They are told that all of their problems will go away because someone loves them dearly. Even if their problems stay the same or get worse, they are told that it is to be expected and the full extent of their god's plan is about to unfold and their issues are about to be fixed. Even if they see no end to their troubles and if they are really abandoned, they are told that they will eventually be reimbursed at the end and in the next life where they are going to live like kings and queens. Now, imagine that. Imagine that you are literally waiting to see the almighty's hands of full justice wipe out all of your enemies and take you to your rightful place. If not today, tomorrow. Just wait a little bit longer. Imagine that.

You don't have money? That's okay, because the saviour would be your money. He or she is carefully looking after you although you might not be able to see it at the moment. He or she works in mysterious ways, you know!

Is your heart broken? Have no fear! You will be compensated for it in the next life. Fully!

Did your beloved father or mother pass away? That's alright too. You will certainly see them soon and will be reunited with them for ever.

In light of these hopes and promises and carefully crafted ways of dodging and hiding the contradictions and problems, the religions are able to thrive like there is no tomorrow.

Now, you tell me. What does atheism and atheists' speeches, books, talks, and works have generated to be able to even remotely challenge those deeply rooted and highly polished methods of persuasion? I will tell you: Nothing!

There is no question about those hopes, promises, fears, and the rest being all empty and fake. There is no question that they can easily be debunked and shown to be fraudulent and empty as it is done all over the world by brilliant atheists. There is no doubt that those hopes will eventually turn out to be nothing but wishful thinking and the promises will never come to pass. There is no question about any of those, and they can be debunked in a case by case fashion.

But, that is not my point. My point is that religions actually use these techniques to hold people's minds hostage for as long as they can. And they are incredibly good at doing so. They cheat, make up false stories and false testimonies, forge letters[24], they lie, they kill to get the job done, they pretend, they scare and terrorise, they burn people at the stake, they do everything in their power to establish and keep their iron fists around the lives of every human being. They commit the most horrendous, unethical acts to stay in power and to get their hands into your pocket and mine (e.g. Osho, Sai Baba, etc.).

I am not suggesting that atheists also should use those methods to advance their point of view. They must not and they cannot.

I am suggesting that the battle atheists are fighting is against a beast and most atheists don't show any clear sign of understanding the magnitude and the weight of it.

Atheists in their works, books, speeches, and words are everything that most religious authors are not. They are honest, up front, seeking only truth even if it will be to their disadvantage, they debunk lies instead of create them, unravel myths instead of making them up, try to inform instead of trying to hold back critical information, invite to peace and complain about wars instead of urging to join holy wars, Jihads, and Crusades, demystify scary darknesses instead of instigate images of imaginary bogeymen, monsters, and eternal torturers to scare. Atheists in their works fight for freedom of humanity and equality of all races, genders, ages, and nations instead of holding one nation as *the* chosen nation of imaginary gods, telling men that women are their seeding fields and are worth as much as half the price of the left testicle of a man. And yet, none of these counts.

Why not? Because, it is not the truth that matters to most people of the earth. It is not reality that counts to them. People, human beings, live most of their lives while sleeping, and a great part of the time that they are not in beds, they are still day-dreaming. Humans have a mental life aside from the real, physical world that is as influential in what they do and who they are as the physical world. This mental dream is even more important than reality to most people. And what does atheism do to appeal to that part of the life of human beings? Very little, if anything at all.

I am well aware that we can argue this case for the rest of the life of the universe and demonstrate that a real life, the life of truth, reality, honesty, morality, and peace is a better life, more productive life, and will lead to a much better mental health[25]. We can repeat that mantra until we are blue in the face. But, that will not work if the immediate benefits of such a wonderful medicine is not at all obvious or felt.

Atheism has a thousand and one benefits alright. Who in his or her right mind can genuinely deny those benefits, right? Do you want to know the answer to the last question? Here it is: Almost all religious believers.

They can deny it because they cannot see it immediately. They can deny it because they cannot feel it immediately. Because it sounds, feels, and looks intimidating, cold, and uninviting.

Our faithful fellow human beings can easily deny it because it does not speak to them. It cannot and never tried to have a heart-to-heart conversation with them. It never tried. It never even pretended to try.

This is not a successful strategy by any stretch of imagination. Quite the opposite: It is a sure receipt for failure. If there is only one thing sure about the way atheism is advocated and proposed to the faithfuls, it is that it will fail miserably. It will fall flat on its face from the get go. It is a still-born child. It has no chance to even begin a fair competition. One cannot open the first session of a mathematics class of first-graders by saying: "Hello morons!"

No obligation

> "Our vanity is hardest to wound when our pride has just been wounded."[22]
> — Nietzsche

No one, at all and under any circumstance, is obliged to listen to a jerk. No matter how smart what he says is and no matter how true his propositions are, still they are coming from a jerk and that is enough for many to dismiss them with a wide brush.

If you hear a message of love, along with the request to spare your change, in your holy building of worship, then you will hear, only, the message of love. This is a trade secret that the people of religions have learned long time ago; a few thousand years ago to be precise.

When you are saturated by the message of hope and love and your mind is filled with the words regarding the infinite, universal love of your saviour just for you (while your bank account is emptied at the same time by the same people), you will only remember what is put into your mind, not what is taken out of your bank account.

Then, when you suddenly are confronted by an asshole who tells you who you really are—a gullible, simple-minded, fool—you are not likely to keep listening to that person. You might actually be a fool. But that is not what you know of yourself. You know yourself as a person for whom a god or a goddess has made a special plan. That is who you are told you are. That is who you believe you are. If you are to believe the jerk or your pastor now, you definitely believe the pastor. There won't be any doubt about it, and why should there be?

If you are exposed to a bunch of people throughout your life who would hold your hands, cry with you, pray with you, support you emotionally when you are down and broken, tell you that everything is going to be alright and you are the selected and the saved, and you will eventually be able to see it even if not right now, then it would be unlikely that you will ever bother listening to someone whose first assumption is that you are a moron, a fool, mislead, misinformed, played-with, and unintelligent person. You won't listen to that person.

No one is under the obligation to be informed that he or she is an ignorant monkey.

What have the atheism literature done so far to ameliorate this impression? What message of love, emotional support, and hope for future has an atheist given to a religious believer? When was the last time that an atheist has held your hand, cried with you, told you all the good things that you need to hear to feel better, not once and accidentally, but on a regular basis?

Atheists are as nice as any theist can ever be. They are as supportive, as helpful, and hopeful, and as humane as the best theist and even better. But, when it comes to converting anyone to freedom, they have not been able to do a good job yet.

The atheism literature cannot compete with the theistic literature in providing the sort of comfort that people need in their daily lives with their problems or successes. There is no obligation on anyone to listen to an inferior system of persuasion that does not work the way it is advertised at first and is not marketed the same way their own tried-and-true pills are marketed to them for years. Atheists have a serious marketing issue and a troubling PR crisis on their hands.

You can teach someone something by humiliating them once. But, in all likelihood, you will never get a second chance to teach them another lesson again. Your tutelage is finished!

Atheists are happy

Of course atheists are going to be absolutely happy with yet another religion-bashing book that is released into the market. Of course, they will praise it, even if it never adds anything of value to the discussion; just because it is a necessary move. Of course atheists will clap their hands off after a hotly-discussed public talk by another atheist because they think he or she has taught the theists a great lesson.

All the signals and signs are telling the same story: That atheists are content with the way things are, and they even think that they are succeeding.

But, they are actually not winning, if not losing indeed. What they are doing, in reality, is to provide yet another push behind the mental moves of people who have already taken the first steps by themselves.

That is not winning. That is not enlightening in the strong sense of it.

The deeply religious fellow who is searching for truth and is trying to find the hows and whys of his doubts about his religion's dogma, is already enlightened. The crucial first step has already been taken.

If a person who is progressively asking more and more questions about the religion he has grown up with comes across a very well-written atheistic literature and finds the way out of the maze of the dogma, he is not won over by reason through *that* literature. He or she is most likely using the best-practice reasoning techniques, whether he knows it or not, and the literature only provides the final push. The final push is important, but it can happen, and would happen, more often than not without the help of a very well-written piece of secular literature anyway.

That is not winning hearts of our fellow humans. That is not a win at all. It might be a win at showing the best or the shortest path to someone out of darkness. However, that is merely showing the path to someone who would have found her path out of darkness with or without that help, sooner or later, anyway. That is not a win I am concerned about.

Don't get me wrong. The literature of atheism is beyond being fabulous. But, it is completely ineffective when it comes to the art of persuasion. It sucks at it.

It persuades the already persuaded very well. It brilliantly informs the already informed. It communicates flawlessly with those who already tuned their hearts and minds on its frequencies. Nevertheless, although the tune is playing from the radio, it totally sucks at gaining new ears from those who don't listen to radios. It sucks incredibly at attracting the attention of those for whom most of these material is supposedly composed. It falls on deaf ears, does not provide any hearing aid, and therefore cannot communicate as it should. The atheism literature and the atheist communities do not cater to most techniques for winning the hearts of the faithful fellow humans.

For some reason, they are also proud of it too, as if that has always been the purpose of the talks they give, the books they write, and the words they spread. They take an overblown pride in not being flexible, not yielding, not accommodating, and not bending at all before any religious mind or idea. They are being assertive and that is that. They are happy with that.

Well, that is not only an unintelligent outlook of the reality of the world that some of them hold, but also a very disappointing one too. It is unintelligent because it is not winning any new minds at all. Disappointing, because it discourages those minds that might have had a brighter future otherwise had they not been encountered by those unintelligent confrontations. It damages more than it fixes.

Denial

> ""I have done that," says my memory. "I cannot have done that," says my pride, and remains inexorable. Eventually—memory yields."[22]
> — Nietzsche

When confronted with this obvious and testable fact that many defenders of atheism indeed offend their opponents instead of persuading them, some of the offenders actually deny the charge completely. They believe that this has never happened. They argue that since they have not seen it happening, and since I or other objectors have not given them concrete examples, therefore it does not exist.

The problem with this approach is that first of all it is completely nonsensical and untrue.

> "— Atheist Experience: The author of this one [i.e. Atheist Experience] says I don't give specific examples, and therefore because he hasn't seen the insults they don't exist... and then accuses *me* of a strawman argument! I find that funny; finding examples about which I was speaking is trivially easy. The author also says I set up a false dichotomy and call people who don't agree with me dicks... all without the benefit of having heard my talk. I talk *specifically* about people who are insulting and demeaning, and talk at length about passion and not backing down. Yet he seems to think I am calling for everyone to not be passionate.

I'm not. I'm calling for them not to be dicks. As far as appealing to emotion... hello! *It's an emotional issue.* **That's the point.** Note that my appeal to emotion was logical because it sets up my premise that being a dick doesn't help. Again, I don't tell people to simply back down from a fight. I just don't think we need to insult our opponent."[16]

There are a few serious dangers in this. One is that because the claim that it never happened is a delusion, it gives the impression that not only the offenders do offend (because it is easy to come across many examples at any given time), but also they deny it too. So, two vices in one move.

The other danger is that it might give the impression that the offenders are morons, for they might be honestly thinking, falsely of course, that what they claim is true, while it is totally false. So, they might be innocent fools who are incapable of seeing the most obvious things around them. What a big blind-spot!

In either case, denying the existence of the issues mentioned above is not the solution. It actually adds to the problem.

The measure of success

Of course not all atheist are making these mistakes and not all atheistic literature is crap. If we exclude the goal of speaking to the heart of religious people to make them think and make them choose the right path, then most of the literature is actually phenomenal. But, if we take into account that a lot of these talks, conversations, conferences, books, workshops, forums, and groups are build to demystify the stone-age myths and to inform people and to eliminate religiosity, and to make religious people abandon their dogmas, then we will see how badly they are performing at the moment.

The measure of success of a public talk to persuade religious mind that they are not on the right side of the equation is not the number of *atheists* who attend the talk, nor the number of books that are sold outside of the conference room with the fans of the speaker, and not the number of tickets that are sold to those who are dying to attend that particular speaker's talk. This is the measure of a different kind of success. If the purpose of the talk has been to gather as many *atheist* as possible, and to sell books to as many *atheists* as possible, and sell out all tickets a few months in advance to the fans and fellow *atheists*, then yes. It could be a big success if those things happen.

But, if the goal has been to win over the minds and the hearts of *theists*, to make them agreeable, to pull them into reality from their fantasy world, to inform them and such, then those numbers and measures actually are not useful.

For the latter causes, instead, the measure of success would be different. How many *theists* have fallen in love with your message? How many *theists* waited in lines to buy your books? How many *theists* have bought your ticket and purchased a few extra for their beloved ones to bring them over to your talk? How many bouquets of flowers you got from the *theists*?

Yeah! You got the idea!

Immaturity of the atheism movement cannot be made any more obvious than this. It hasn't been doing it. It doesn't know how to do it. It doesn't know *that* it should have been doing it. So, it is in a compounded state of ignorance: It doesn't know that it doesn't know the trick. This is not a good sign at all.

A taste of your own medicine

"How does it taste so far, you idiot?" Imagine me telling my fellow atheists. "This is the taste of your own medicine. This is how it tastes when you call others names. You, moron, could not see it till now. Because you haven't had enough intelligence to see it on your own and have been living, rather comfortably, in a cocoon of your making. Your books are only good for yourself and your own like-minded friends, you delusional soul. Wake up! This is not how to communicate. We should work on your communication skill dumb-ass. Smart up! At least try to learn something from your opponents. Are you that dumb? Ummm... I am actually not surprised."

How did it taste so far? Not that yummy, eh? I bet not! But this is exactly the tone you hear in many the atheism communities when they are trying to enlighten a theist. To that, I would say, to hell with all of the atheists and theists alike!

It doesn't taste good right? So far, I have been criticising you almost in your own tone and telling you how you miserably fail left and right, my atheist friends. And as you can see and feel, it doesn't feel great to be talked down to like this. But I am going to keep going, using the same methodology, to inform you of your shortcomings. Because, it has a few benefits. On the one hand, it demonstrates to you, in real-time, how it is to be brutally criticised and therefore gives you a bit of your own medicine to taste. And on the other hand, it actually reminds you of the severity and the emergency of the problem in hand. Atheists are less used to be handed over sugar-coated, idle remarks, and are a lot more likely to see the truth through the bitter taste of this criticism. So, it is better to keep it simple, clean, and brutal. I am talking to atheists after all and am not going to win them over anything. I just want them to see the issue as clearly as possible. They are equipped with enough mental tools to dismantle my brutal voice and get what is worth paying attention to and what should be discarded. Most fellow religious humans need some work in that department and that is why they would have turned away from a tone such as this. So, I should not have a big problem with atheists.

Anyway, when you read this book, if you felt bad at any time, because I was right and you were wrong, or because I made sense and you didn't, keep a notebook by yourself and jot down your feelings and my tone at that moment. Then try to see if I couldn't have said it in a different tone (hint: I certainly could have).

The cost of lost opportunities

> "It is terrible to die of thirst in the ocean. Do you have to salt your truth so heavily that it does not even—quench thirst any more?"[22]
> — Nietzsche

This unnecessary and futile fight that some movements within atheism are involved in have an enormous cost to the society and the human civilization in general. I would say it is as immoral, albeit unintentionally so, as any foolish act that might damage the society.

In economics, there is something called opportunity cost: "the loss of potential gain from other alternatives when one alternative is chosen."[26] Or put it in a different way:

> "Simply stated, an opportunity cost is the cost of a missed opportunity. It is the opposite of the benefit that would have been gained had an action, not taken, been taken—the missed opportunity."[27]

> "An opportunity cost is defined as the value of a forgone activity or alternative when another item or activity is chosen. Opportunity cost comes into play in any decision that involves a tradeoff between two or more options. It is expressed as the relative cost of one alternative in terms of the next-best alternative."[28]

According to this concept, every time that a religious fellow human is offended by an atheist, a great opportunity is lost, damage is caused, and a future possibility is blocked. The chances are that the offended person goes even a few steps backward.[19]

Not only this is a huge cost to the society where that person lives, but also this is a potential cost and damage to our civilization. We never know who we have lost to a foolish strategy. He or she could have been a great asset, a brilliant force of good against human gullibility that now is rendered almost unobtainable.

Also, we don't know what the damage might bring up in the person. It might make her a worse person. It might make her more adamant in her way and more resistant to any positive change.[19]

Another cost is through the self-imposed deprivation that now is even more encouraged by being negatively impacted. Instead of the dialogue resulting in freeing the person from superstitions and faith, it results in pushing the faithful deeper into the hole where they are stuck in. This deprives the person from all the benefits of a secular life, from the pure morality and high ethical values that accompany a secular life compared to the corrupted and conditional morality that religions advocate, and from the health benefits that come with the atheistic point of view compared to a religious one.[25]

If we do not, or cannot, or refuse to, recognize these as costs, we are doomed to repeat the same mistakes that religions are making: Imposing unnecessary costs on human societies and civilizations, whereas it is something that can be avoided with intelligent planning and the good-will of the atheist community and individuals.

Jerry DeWitt style

Jerry DeWitt is a person who seriously got me thinking about the way atheism is advocated. Atheism starts with emphasising on conflicts and contradictions. It starts tense and ends more tense. Jerry, a very successful ex-pastor, uses his skills to have honest conversations in a very different way. He does not start with conflicts, nor does he mention the contradictions in the Bible right away. His way of doing things is different. It is ironic that we have to learn from religion to know how to fight against religion.

There are many videos of Jerry talking to an audience at different conferences, gatherings, and even to the camera. A search on YouTube will bring up a bunch of them. If you are not sure about his style, start from one of his earliest videos at:

http://youtu.be/zpmvIxfqYmY (please remember that the link is case-sensitive).[29] It gives you an idea about his style of talking.

The approach he is taking is almost entirely opposite of what many atheists take to advance their noble cause. He starts with including everyone whereas many atheists start with a big division that separates them from the theists. Jerry brings himself down to the level of his audience while many atheists sound pretentious in their conversations as if they are there to show off the depth and the extends of their knowledge to their opponents. Jerry sees the theists as his fellow men and women, neighbours, his best friends, and so on with many of whom he has fine memories. Many atheists denounce theists as if they are from a different planet. Jerry deeply and genuinely sympathizes with his audience at every level whereas many defenders of atheism try to distance themselves from theists as if they have nothing to do with them, and they are nothing and nobody to them. Jerry still loves many of his religious friends for good reason, and he says so, but some atheists come across as if becoming an atheist must necessarily mean that you have to hate your old religious friends. The differences are many. You must watch a few of his videos to see him for yourself.

Of course, he is accused of preaching as he used to as a pastor. Nevertheless, if that is the price one must pay to enlighten others, then let be it.

WRITING ABOUT ATHEISM WITH RELIGIOUS MINDS IN MIND

> "The more abstract the truth is that you would teach, the more you have to seduce the senses to it."[22]
> — Nietzsche

I have never been a pastor. I know that they have culminated a few thousand years of experience with persuading others of the most absurd, unacceptable, and false ideas. Many of them know the how-tos. The other side of the fence, i.e. atheists, usually do not know any of these trade secrets.

The first thing that we need to do is to admit that we can do much better. We have some catching-up do regarding our conversation techniques.

Then we should study the correct way of having a genuine conversation with a person who probably suspects all of our moves. Religions are inherently mistrustful of every outsider. They are mistrustful of their motives. Religions also are scared of the consequences of listening to an outsider should his arguments make a dent in the system they have carefully built. Add the universal cognitive dissonance to all of these and you will have a tough nut to crack.

Denial

Now let us study denial from the believers' perspective. According to The Gale Encyclopedia of Mental Disorders, "**denial**" is: "the refusal to acknowledge the existence or severity of unpleasant external realities or internal thoughts and feelings."[30]

If you confront a believer with facts and reality, the first thing that you will cause in her is to set her back into a deep state of denial. Since religions have promised incredible things, things that are not possible to happen in reality, they have raised the expectations of impressionable people. Believers genuinely believe and wants to stick to the dream of those promises coming true. In many cases, reality says otherwise. That is a huge conflict right away at the doorstep.

On the one hand, reality sets limits to what is possible and gives hints of what is impossible. Logic, on the other hand, sets hard limits to what can or cannot be done. Physical reality combined with logical possibilities prohibits the occurrence of certain events at all time for all observers everywhere in the universe. That is a 'forever' prohibition in some cases. Such a forever-prohibition might not come to a believer as a "good news" per se. The fact that one will not see one's beloved, deceased friends or family members can be seen as a devastating blow to their emotional stability. No one in their right mind would expose themselves to such perceived attacks.

The reality can actually be perceived as scary, cold, unpleasant, and unwelcoming. When we talk to a religious friend or family member, they usually complain about their lives becoming pointless and purposeless if they stop believing in their brand of religion. That is a good-enough justification for most of them to cling to the myths they happened to grow up with. Without the tale, they say that they will be lost. It is the story, the tale, or the dream-world that gives structure to their thoughts and emotions. They drive their personal purpose, the point for staying alive, from these stories. Or they think they are.

Telling them that after demolishing their current house of cards, we won't be able to recommend the right course of action to them, and they are the ones who need to find their own way of life and their own purpose in life is not reassuring. This makes them anxious and even more uncertain about the path we might be proposing them to take. From the outset, this equals to them trading everything they have been collecting in their current path with the hope of getting to know reality more intimately. This is not an enticing prospect for most people. "Reality?" What the heck is that good for if it is going to disturb or potentially evaporate everything I have collected in my life through my religion? My dreams will go, my hopes will go, most of my friends will leave me, my church will go, and my life would turn upside down. Why should I take that risk? What for?

Not everyone cares about truth and reality in the same way that not everyone is a philosopher. Reality and truth, for most people, are what is in their favour. You cannot market 'reality' or 'truth' to religious minds. These are rare commodities that they won't buy and are told to distrust. Most religions claim, implicitly or explicitly, that reality is an illusion and must be avoided at all cost. "The 'real' reality comes in the life after," they would say. You cannot sell the idea of reality or truth to someone whose valuation of reality and truth is close to zero.

What happens next when we ignore these facts and bring up the issues of reality and truth in conversations is that we put our audience on defensive. They go into a deep state of denial right away and all subsequent attempts to keep a meaningful conversation with them will be closed off from this point on. If it occurs early in a conversation, then you have already lost the cause.

Shouldn't we talk about our beliefs and their relationships with reality eventually at some point then? Yes, we should. There is no way to avoid that topic. However, if our listeners are immediately put into a defensive mode in the beginning of a conversation, there won't be a good point down the road to introduce anything, because the ears are closed already.

Most religious people have already decided on whether they want to see reality as it is. They have made up their minds. They already know well what it means for the real world being different from their dream-world. They know the differences, and they don't like it. They already know that it could emotionally cost them dearly if they let go of their ancient myths. In most cases, the cost is usually way too high. They cannot even begin to imagine what they need to sacrifice to see the world as it really is.

The cost of switching is often high, the effort to make it happen is often charged emotionally, the road is uncertain and seems uninviting, the task sounds daunting, and to many ordinary people 'monumental'. The incentives seem vague at best and non-existent at worst. Any possible confrontation has the potential of increasing the believers' denial level.

Cognitive dissonance

This goes hand in hand with the mental denial function. *International Encyclopedia of the Social Sciences* mentions a few important elements regarding the mechanism of cognitive dissonance:

> "Cognitive dissonance is [...] describing the way in which people cope with and rationalize inconsistencies in their experience, such as holding incompatible beliefs, acting in ways that violate their values, being forced to choose one of two equally attractive alternatives, or discovering that their efforts were not worth the result obtained. The term refers both to a lack of harmony among one's thoughts and to the discomfort that results from this, which individuals are motivated to reduce by

changing their mind or their behavior in the service of greater cognitive consonance. From its initial focus on discordant thoughts, the theory has evolved over the years to stress that the ultimate motivation for reducing dissonance is to preserve the belief that one is a good and rational person, and the theory is now primarily used to understand processes by which individuals justify past behavior to themselves."[31]

I am going to list the crucial elements in this definition to understand the challenge we face when we engage in a conversation with a believer.

So, cognitive dissonance usually occurs when the person we talk to starts to *think* that:

- we imply that they are holding incompatible beliefs;
- accepting our position makes them act in ways that violate their values;
- we might have forced her to choose one of two equally attractive alternatives;
- we are telling her that her religious efforts were all in vain; and
- we strongly suggested that she is not a good and rational person.

What else do you need to make them feel the total force of cognitive dissonance?

When this happens, her entire being starts to react to the perceived threats to reduce the terrible emotions caused by the "facts" and the "reality." What you can bring to the table next is indeed irrelevant. By causing cognitive dissonance a speaker can seal the fate of a conversation from the moment it triggers the reaction.

It seems that one of the more effective ways of going about having a Socratic dialogue with a believer is to appeal to their goodness and rationality, in spite of the fact that most of what they believe is either false, based on fallacious arguments, or unsupported by any reproducible evidence. The fact of the matter is that most, if not all, people do have a rational side and are capable of doing good. Appeal to these realities instead of starting from a losing end.

Inclusion, control, affection

Working with someone to let go of his worst nightmares and step out of his dark corner into the real world requires a lot of teamwork. Consider yourself a midwife to help your religious fellow human to come to the realization that the real world actually exists and it might be different from what their religion dogma had made them to believe. Socrates described himself as a midwife who was helping other to give birth to noble and truthful ideas.

> [...]
> SOCRATES: Such are the midwives, whose task is a very important one, but not so important as

> mine; for women do not bring into the world at one time real children, and at another time counterfeits which are with difficulty distinguished from them; if they did, then the discernment of the true and false birth would be the crowning achievement of the art of midwifery—you would think so?
> THEAETETUS: Indeed I should.
> SOCRATES: Well, my art of midwifery is in most respects like theirs; but differs, in that I attend men and not women; and look after their souls when they are in labour, and not after their bodies: and the triumph of my art is in thoroughly examining whether the thought which the mind of the young man brings forth is a false idol or a noble and true birth. [...][32]

Ironically, Socrates got a death sentence for what he was doing, so don't assume that you are going to be on the safe side just by acting as if your are a midwife for ideas. It might not work all the time!

Pretending to be helping and actually helping someone to arrive at a realization are two different things. Humans have evolved with a neat set of fake-detectors. They are good at telling when a person is merely pretending to help and when they actually are helping. So, you need to devise a genuine and honest strategy to enable others to understand reality and make them capable to live with the consequences. Realizing that it is your duty as a citizen to help other citizen to have better lives might change your attitude.

Approach every individual as an end not as a means. Each individual must be respected as a person regardless of their personal convictions. This is the attitude of all courts even when they are dealing with criminals. It is not because anyone likes criminals. It is because by hurting the dignity of a human being we also hurt the dignity of all human being, and that should not be acceptable anywhere. The dignity of a criminal as a human being must always be respected. This is only an example. Here we are not talking about criminals. Here we are talking about our brothers and sisters, mothers and fathers, classmates, neighbours, lovers, girlfriends and boyfriends, colleagues and co-workers, teachers, students, drivers, and everyone we might come across in our daily lives. Their dignity must be respected.

To work with these people, i.e. all the believers in our lives, we need to think of them as our team members. It might not be easy at first but it will become your second nature if you practice several times. To secure the cooperation of your team members, you need to make them feel that they are included in your team. Inclusion is the key to their successful cooperation, their happiness, and their growth.

The aim of enlightening religious people is to make them grow, to make them better, to make them happier, and to make them more successful. It can only be done if we can earn their trust and keep it. They also must be included in the process. They must feel that they are part of it, not its puppet.

"[...] Three interpersonal needs are especially central to securing people's commitment within workgroups and teams:
Inclusion—a sense of being recognized, involved, and accepted;
Control—a sense of having a responsible role and of being invited to influence; and
Affection—a sense of being respected, supported, and close to other members of the group."[33]

To succeed in a Socratic dialogue, you should bet your odds on the cooperation of your audience instead of reducing your chance of being heard by instigating confrontations. Remember that the goal of such conversations always is to make the audience grow and learn. If they feel they are taken seriously, and they are part of the conversation, in oppose to being talked to or being passive listeners of a monologue, they will listen. If you show them that you genuinely enjoy having the conversation with them, that you also are learning something new, and that you are on their team, then you will get their attention and sympathy.

Again, you can see how all of these elements exist in Jerry's style and are absent from most atheists' conversation styles.

> All credibility, all good conscience, all evidence of truth come only from the senses.[22]
> — Nietzsche

If you are pleasant to the ears and warm towards the hearts, you increase your chances of being heard. Unless you are heard, your passion for educating believers will not bear fruits; not as much as it should.

Universal love

> "Chien-ai
> A term coined by the Warring States philosopher Mo-tzu, referring to universal love. From Mo-tau's point of view, there should be no differentiation in love between people—it should be shown equally whether one is a close relative or a stranger, a senior or a junior. Universal love, it was believed, could smooth away differences between people and states, leading to peace in the world. Mo-tzu was very critical of the Confucians for engaging in what he referred to as partial love—love graduated on a scale of specialness of relationship. He argued that love with discrimination only preserved a hierarchy of relationships, not the promotion of a truly moral world."[34]

How true is that! Unfortunately, universal love is usually only talked about and then neglected. It is not the same as "love your enemy" because that is often immoral if not impossible.[35] As Xunzi would have said, loving everyone in the world is neither practical nor realistic.[36] It is also not "love thy neighbour" either since this piece in the Bible actually refers to the children of thy people, which are fellow Israelites; not universal at all.[35]

Considering those qualifications, an advocate of atheism should always remember why they do what they do. They are not advocating atheism merely for fun, although it might be fun at times too. They are doing it because they love humanity in general. They hate ignorance. They want as many human beings to be educated as possible. They care about the world, the others, and the ones they engage in friendly conversations. They want everyone around them to live a happy, fulfilled, and beautiful lives. Otherwise, there is no point in spreading the truth about the world. They get into trouble and go out of their way to help others. This comes because of love and caring.

When one remembers these, then one's attitude and strategies change instantly. There won't be any room for neglect, disrespect, exclusion, in-group/out-group games, pretension, anger, or impatience.

To give you a more tangible example, imagine that you are a grade one teacher who loves his job and loves his students. He would be super patient with them. He would go over simple and often tedious steps with his students repeatedly if needed. He would respect them greatly although they know nothing compared to how much he knows. What kind of feeling, attitude, and methodology do you think he is employing? Whatever your answer would be, that is what you need to employ when you are engaging in a Socratic dialogue with believers.

Know that one of these students might be the next Einstein or the next Marie Curie. You don't know who he or she is, but you know that your responsibilities are huge towards this possibility. What if this very student you are talking to is going to be one of the greatest inventors or discoverers in the history of the human kind? You cannot know and that is why you must take that possibility into account when you are engaging with them.

The same applies to those believers with whom you converse. They can be many times smarter, kinder, more loving, and all-in-all better human being than you are. Let's say you had the chance to get into a deep conversation with Jerry DeWitt when he still was a pastor and has not come to the realization that he finally came to. Let's say you saw him in year 1995. Could you tell if he was going to become one of the best and brightest atheists on this planet? One of the kindest? One of the most influential? I bet you couldn't. Heck, I bet my life on that! You could not have guessed, in your wildest dreams that he would eventually realize the vanity of religions and would become the person he is today. In hindsight, you should have talked to him with utmost respect.

Now, extrapolate this thought experiment to the rest of the people on earth. You are always at this crossroad. Every day is a day you engage with someone who might go down the history as a true hero, as a great person, and an atheist. Every conversation, potentially, is a conversation with a Jerry DeWitt in 1995. So treat all of them as such.

Rush

When you have a conversation with a believer, the focus of the task is to engage them emotionally and intellectually.

The intellectual part of it is the easy part. There are so many examples, evidence, and arguments based on facts and experiences against religious claims that it is virtually a matter of taste to pick one and present it to your listener. There are mountains of evidence that refute most claims made by every religion at every turn of every debate. Of course there are unfalsifiable claims made by religions all over the place, and they are, by their nature, not falsifiable that makes them completely useless and arbitrary. However, the claims that are falsifiable have been falsified repeatedly to the point of triviality. So, the intellectual challenge is actually not that much challenging after all.

The emotional part, though, is the hardest part and the step that must be taken with utmost care and attention. This element of engagement, i.e. emotions, is fragile and easy to mess up. Causing suspicion and distrust is almost effortless. Getting your audience defensive does not need any wit or expertise. Start your conversation with 'how different atheism is from the world-view that your listener is currently entertaining' and you are already set. They will immediately get defensive and that would be the end of your journey through your dialogue. As such, there won't be any dialogue left any more.

To avoid making your listener feel excluded, emotionally attacked, and intellectually challenged, you need to keep the emotional aspect of your conversation in mind all the time; not occasionally, but constantly. To do so, you have to be genuine and look and sound genuine.

However, one sure way to screw up the whole setting is to rush through the emotional elements to get to the intellectual points. This makes the journey look fake. It is easy to think of the emotional element as a stage you have to get through and be done with before you can get to the meaty part of your intellectual conversation. Nothing can be farther from truth than this.

The emotional element of a conversation is the foundation, the context if you wish, in which the conversation should occur. A stage or a stepping stone to pass over or pass by, it is not. You are not going to be able to fully detach the emotional elements from any conversation you might have with believers, or with any other listener for that matter. Only in very rare cases a conversation can be had with nearly zero amount of emotions being evoked. There won't be any moment during your dialogue with a believer that you can assume that you are done and over with the emotional elements. It won't happen, ever.

Therefore, be watchful of every step you are taking. Know that you are always walking on eggshells. Always!

Rushing through any number of comforting reassurances merely to do your duty to finish the hard part of the puzzle, is wrong at many levels. The positive atmosphere for which your uttered words would be partially responsible is not a scene that has a beginning and an end. Nor is it a puzzle you need to solve. Effective human interaction is a skill and a necessity through all stages of a constructive dialogue.

Emotional interference

Positive emotions are not mere means to an end. They are ends in themselves. The intellectual elements would be discarded or ignored altogether if the context inside of which they are presented is hostile. It doesn't matter how factual, real, and truth any proposition might be. As long as it causes negative emotions in listeners, it will face impenetrable walls to bore through. By rushing a conversation based on a mistaken conception of emotional engagement, one can ruin the possibility of having fruitful conversations. Be patient and pleasant all the way from A to Z.

> Use soft words and hard arguments.
> — Anonymous

The emotional elements are usually every bit as important as the intellectual elements. The intellectual elements are rejected or not properly considered *because of* the interference of the emotional elements. As I said before, the intellectual challenges are pretty easy. They are so easy that we cannot legitimately call them "challenges." As far as facts, reality, and truth are concerned, all religions' cases are closed. What is *not* closed, though, is how emotions get in the way of intellect to block the person from any further investigation into the truth of the matters.

When an atheist starts a conversation with a believer, the first thing that happens is they provoke the emotional firewalls in the minds of the ones they are talking to. Not only do they start an emotional alarm in their mind, but they also raise the sensitivity of their reactions by poking their sensitive mental spots. When it starts to hurt, the pain blocks the communication channels and distracts their focus.

Pain is bad, and emotional pain is the worst. There are studies that show how effective emotional pain is at potentially distracting anyone from doing virtually anything, thinking, staying calm, paying attention, concentrating, caring, making sense, or even staying sane. Chronic emotional pain can easily result in mental wounds that can turn into long-lasting emotional injuries with serious social and interpersonal effects. Healthy people react negatively to emotional pain, but you might not always be dealing with emotionally stable people. According to a study, chronically depressed people will overreact to such emotional threats such as social exclusion.[37]

Social rejection & emotional pain

This belongs to the same set of emotional interferences. Social rejection causes emotional pain. When you are confronting a believer, in opposed to having a Socratic dialogue with them, you are facing at least two aspects of social rejection.

If you confront the believer, then you are explicitly rejecting them. This is hurtful enough and I have already talked about it in some length.

However, if they accept your position they might make themselves exposed to a much greater and serious social rejection from their previous social group, church, synagogue, or even neighbourhood or village. They might even risk losing their jobs, their family members, their marriage, the alliance with their social network, their financial stability, and much more.

Jerry DeWitt had an interview sometime after his announcement of being an atheist in May 20th, 2012. In there he tells the audience the challenges he faced and the huge sacrifices that he needed to make to 'get out of the closet'.[38]

About a year later Jerry had another speech, this time accompanied by Dan Barker, and talked about his journey, which he called 'Life After Faith', and the consequences of his decision in the past couple of years. You can see and evaluate the enormity of the cost that he incurred to stand where he was standing in the latter conference.[39]

When you are watching those videos, pay close attention to the evolution of his situation, the cost of his actions, the emotional price he had to pay, and the troubles he had to go through. In one sense, it is like he kicked himself out of his own life by his own foot.

If you ever think that coming to see what reality is and letting go of religions' myths can be as simple as reading a book by Richard Dawkins or listening to a debate between Christopher Hitchens and Tony Blair, you certainly have a lot of homework to do! Indeed, this attitude is the root of most problems that atheists cause when they try to "help" believers with their inputs. You cannot watch those videos and still believe that letting go of irrational beliefs is only a matter of reading a few books or paying close attention to your well-formed arguments.

Actually, you might come out as a different person, a bit more pessimistic indeed, after observing the struggles that Jerry has had during his journey. His troubles seem to keep coming and at some point he seems to be desperate and deeply distressed to his core.

When you hear his story, you will realize that, maybe, just maybe, all it takes is phenomenal and extraordinary courage. Not intellectual power, nor factual knowledge, not even logic seem to be instrumental enough to change a believer's mind. What does make a huge difference, you may realize, might be the psychological stamina and the social forces that usually work against a person even entertaining the possibility of abandoning their faith.

The social rejection when a person announces her final thoughts on the vanity of religious beliefs can potentially be utterly devastating. Because of this possibility, you always must carefully assess the situation on a case-by-case basis and intercept the possible gains and costs associated with accepting or rejecting your position. If the gains sound vague, far-fetched, not immediate, and the losses are multifaceted, long-lasting, immediate, obvious, and painful to handle, you will need a long-term, expanded strategy if you ever hope to free a believer from the shackles of the religion they are clinging to.

> "It is difficult to free fools from the chains they revere."
> — Voltaire

By the way, I don't recommend reciting this quotation to your believer friends either. It is for your own information only!

The ramifications of socially disturbing behaviours, such as denouncing the religion of your fathers, can be so damaging that most rational humans won't consider acceptable, practical, or reasonable. Rationality is not the same as truthfulness. A rational position in a particular social setting might require one to pretend they belong to a group of people while they privately know that they don't. This shouldn't be surprising. We are social animals after all and social events do affect our well-beings, and we do take them into account seriously. Social conformity can be so pressing that it can disable the individual's desire to think freely or to dissociate from the group in which they are embedded.

Even if you can persuade a person of facts and the evidence against his false beliefs, that does not necessarily mean that he will jump into your boat right away and will abandon his already-established social setting. If anything, such an event would be highly improbable. It might only happen once or twice in anyone's life that one changes his or her mind abruptly as a result of a sudden eureka moment. You even might not see it with your own eyes. So, don't bet your odds on that to happen in any of your Socratic dialogues with your believer audiences.

What you should expect, instead, is to form enduring alliances with those you deeply care about—which should be almost everyone—as much as you can. You want to be a part of their social setting and work with them to get them out of the dream-world into reality. Have a conversation *with* them and not against them. Build a strong social connection with them and avoid making them feel rejected or humiliated. Minimize even the possibility of them thinking that they necessarily need to sacrifice a great deal to privately come to a realistic conclusion about reality. Don't make them pay an unexpected emotional price up-front.

Alternatives

When a social network breaks down, most of its benefits also disappear. The emotional support that used to be shared with the affected person simply vanishes. The person might find himself being left alone, high and dry to his own demise. In many cases, the consequences of realizing the reality of religions go beyond emotional injuries. Jerry's case shows us what other consequences might be waiting for the person down the road and how severe they might be.

Imagine that you lost your job, your spouse, most of your friends, the house you could finally afford to buy (and now cannot pay its mortgage because you lost your spouse who used to pay half of the fees), and your grandma's blessing. Add to that the realization that you are damned by almost everyone in your town, no one gives you a job any more, no one even wants to see you any more, and your family is about to implode as a result of your recent announcement that you don't believe in the tales of your ex-religion any longer. How would you be feeling then? What would you like to hear from others? How do you want others to react to these catastrophic events that are unfolding in your life?

Under such a tremendous distress, most humans need a shoulder to cry on to begin with. When the initial shock wave pass and the severe pain of these losses give way to a constant, chronic, emotional pain of the realization that one's life has all been wasted in vain. That one needs to restructure their life around the reality of the situation that has just unfolded before their eyes. This requires a lot of planning and good management skills that most people might not readily posses. This is when any help can be dearly appreciated by the affected person.

We can't properly realize the severity of the situation unless we, personally, have gone through a similar hurricane and come out in one piece. Even hearing about it from someone's mouth is not enough to put our view in the right perspective. It would help, but it won't get us where we need to be able to feel the growing pains of a new atheist in such a condition. What we *can* do is talk to as many new atheists as we can and to listen to as many stories as they can share with us to get a better picture of the circumstance.

When we do our homework, we realize that leaving a newly-freed person on their own to find their way is not an option. We need to also be prepared to be resourceful and come up with alternative plans to ease their transition into the light of a superstition-free world. By "alternative plans" I don't mean answers to cosmological questions. Many cosmological questions either don't have any answer yet, will never have any answer, or have simple answers. I am talking about the collapse of the social, psychological, and emotional world around the ex-believer. What to do with the huge vacuum?

Many support groups are gradually emerging in different cities around the world. The movement is still in its infancy. People are still experimenting with different support mechanisms. New ideas to financially help ex-believers who are now out of their jobs due to their changed understanding of the world are being proposed and attempted. Organizations are being formed to help those in need of emotional or financial support. People are mobilizing their resources to make the consequences of leaving faith behind less painful.

Research these resources and compile a list of charitable organizations and support groups to back up your enlightening plans and to help your friends with their new life.

One very nicely written book that would help you get a good head-start is *A Manual for Creating Atheists* by Peter Boghossian. Many of its chapters close with a list of websites and the names of organizations, people, books, support groups, and places where one can turn to if one needs serious help after transition from faith to reality.[40]

The list of similar resources keep growing, so don't limit yourself to these suggestions. There are several meet-up groups that pop-up every month on social networks that one can join to get face-to-face assistance from like-minded people. There are people in groups organized via Facebook, sometimes dedicated to specific cities or towns, that would happily get together with anyone in need regarding leaving a faith. The alternatives are exponentially growing in number, so the chances are that there would be one or more support groups, made of real people for real people, near anyone to help them with the challenges of leaving any faith especially in western societies. As Peter Boghossian would have said, have the list of your resources handy in case you will need them in a conversation with a friend. You will never know when such a need will arise, so you'd better be prepared.

There might be cases when you realize that there is no support group anywhere near your current location. In such a case consider opening up your own chapter of one of the better-known support organizations in your area. Most secular humanist organizations would be more than happy to put you on their list of support chapters in remote areas of the world. There is, and should be, a sense of pride in being able to contribute to the mental and emotional health of others.

Joining forces with any charitable organization is a noble act. One of these organizations that is mentionworthy is called Recovering From Religion.

> "If you are one of the many people who have determined that religion no longer has a place in their life, but are still dealing with the aftereffects in some way or another, Recovering From Religion (RR) may be just the right spot for you. Many people come to a point that they no longer accept the supernatural explanations for the world around them [...]. It can be difficult to leave religion because family and culture put so much pressure on us to stay and

> pretend to believe the unbelievable. If this is you, we want to help you find your way out. [...] RR has support groups that meet monthly all over the US, with groups starting in Canada, the UK, and Australia, and new faces are always welcomed. [...] We are recovering from every imaginable religion: Baptists, Mormons, Catholics, Jehovah's Witnesses, Hindus, Muslims, Lutherans, Pentecostals, Evangelicals, and many more. We are happy, we are healthy, and we warmly welcome you to a life free of the confines of faith."[41]

This is only one example out of many. There is another related project that is composed of secular registered therapists that can be reached in the US for professional help. It is called The Secular Therapist Project.

> If you are looking for a secular mental health professional, this is the first place to look.[42]

If the believer fears of being socially rejected and having nowhere to turn to, a very good place to start looking for social events amongst like-minded people is meetup.com. A simple search for "humanism" or "secular" in your area will likely bring several results. These groups are all grass-root attempts to form social and emotional support for those who need them. They usually have monthly events (and some even have weekly gatherings). I have personally attended many of these events and can tell you how supportive and resourceful they can be. You, as a free-thinker, might want to research your available options (e.g. the local groups in your town) and keep a record of where they are and how they can be reached. It would be a great idea to carry a summary of the top ten resources you have found so you will always be ready to help.

Emotional needs

After talking about being resourceful and having alternative support plans ready to deploy, it would be appropriate to talk about believers' emotional needs that sometimes lead to clinging to what they know is not true.

Humans like stories.[43,44] Anthropologists and ethnologist have discovered that all cultures that ever existed carry stories about most things in their environments. Stories about how and why events occur and who is behind those occurrences. Speculations abound on why these stories come about and why humans have the tendency to tell them. There are other strange examples too. No one exactly knows why most of us like to listen to some sort of music, why we like dancing, why we enjoy watching a sunset, and why most flowers look beautiful to us. Whatever the causes might be, this is how things are here on earth.

These logically senseless acts are all over the place. We all do them one way or another. They seem to fulfil some of our emotional needs. Take the example of music. In general, there is no meaning in any musical pieces (unless a meaning is assigned to it in advance as a signal for indicating something, which is rare). We certainly enjoy listening to music but enjoyment is not a meaning. Enjoyment or joy cannot be judged as right or wrong, or true or false.

Given these observations, the need for storytelling and story-hearing seems to be universal amongst humans. Children seem to be born with "tell me a story" words on their lips. Some elements of the origin of the earliest religions stem from this need. These stories used to give structure to everyone's life, used to transmit cultural elements, used to carry the wisdom of the earlier generations to the later ones, and used to serve many functions that might not be relevant today.

The tendency to make up stories for almost everything is so entrenched into human psyche that reminds me of how language acquisition has become a part of our biological machines. We are born as language acquisition machines amongst other things and maybe we are also born as story-seeking machines too. The fact that almost every living organism is a pattern-recognition system might give support to this hypothesis. Stories are patterns, either made up or observed. They might have been coming from the same brain systems that equip us with the pattern recognition abilities.

Religions do many things and telling stories is also one of them. Humans have evolved to tell stories and this ability makes them also able to *make up* stories as well. Fiction is nothing new. Fictional stories have been around forever. Do you recall the *Epic of Gilgamesh*? That is almost five thousand years old if not older. When you read the story, it is so rich in imagery, so complex in motifs and story-line, and so sophisticated in the way it is constructed that it leave absolutely no doubt in the reader's mind that stories had been around at least as many years before the epic was written. I cannot imagine that the humans of ten thousand years ago were suddenly so different from the ones that came five thousand years later, so they could not tell any story. That sounds absurd. Actually, when we look at the cave paintings and see how elaborate they are, this time envelope is easily pushed back several times over. Go back 40,000 years and you can still find cave paintings in Europe and Asia that rival the best on offer in the latest auctions in London and Paris today. Many of the cave paintings tell stories.

So, there is this deeply rooted need in humans to tell and to listen to stories, and religions happened to fill in the gap comfortably. Atheists who think religions can be eradicated seem to overlook this fact. The stories are going to be around for as long as humans are around, and, surprise, surprise, religions are going to be around for as long as stories sell, which is forever.

When we realize that religions are not going to go anywhere and why, then we would be a lot more sympathetic towards believers. They are not insane only because they entertain crazy stories. Enjoying crazy stories is universal and is fun. It is not right, wrong, true, or false. The stories themselves are usually crazy, made up, and in many cases very childish and unsophisticated. The mere fact that we, humans, like stories, cannot and ought not to be held against us. We are all in it together, atheists and theists alike.

With this acknowledgement in mind and the recognition that we all do the same, atheists should not blame believers for being human. Because blaming them for liking stories is, indirectly, is like blaming them for being humans. Especially because atheists themselves would then be blameworthy for the exact same reason.

What atheists want to do, instead, is to enable believers to tell true stories from fictional ones, or to remain agnostic when the evidences are not conclusive. That is all what atheists might be legitimately responsible for.

So, as a non-believer, work on the logic of stories instead of the existence of the stories. Had it not been this story, believers would have entertained another one. Making up stories has no limits. Non-believers cannot change this simple fact about human psyche. Period! Get done and over with this realization and don't assume that you are any different.

Non-believers, however, are different in the way they evaluate the veracity of the stories they entertain, unlike the way believers process the same data. Believers tend not to cross-reference the sources or even check the validity of them, be bothered by contradictions or even notice them. They tend to make up extra ad-hoc stories to reduce cognitive dissonance caused by the disparities between their grand stories and reality, underestimate the importance or the subversive effect of lies, false claims, and contradictory evidence, and generally not being that good at induction or deduction.

Believers actually have a lot more problems with inductive logic than they have with deductive logic. Deductive logic is absolute and inevitable. I haven't, yet, met a believer of any kind who could seriously question deductive logic. It is pervasive, conclusive, and terribly clear to the simplest life forms on this planet. Heck, even a non-living machine understands it!

Induction, on the other hand, is a totally different story (pun intended). Induction is what everything we know about everything is based upon. Science and technology is totally reliant upon induction. At the same time, it is really easy to mess up. Unless the concept of 'evidence' is properly understood, no constructive conversation can be held with a believer in the context of an inductive argument.

Therefore, one of the central points of a secular education must be explaining and demonstrating the significance of the induction reasoning and evidence-based propositions. Any claim whatsoever is affected. Even this very claim that all claims are affected! Induction is the key to tell the true stories from the fictional ones. Believers need most help in this department.

The above observations tell us that we should not waste time to attack stories *per se*, but the underlying logic of them. Don't disrespect your audience because they are humans, and they need to tell and hear stories for whatever reason. Teach them how to tell fictions from facts. But in order to know how to teach them that skill, you need to first know how to do it yourself. This brings us to the next issue.

The story that we tell ourselves are under the influences of yet another element that can easily distort them and make them totally fictitious. So, it is not only the logic of a story that contributes to its veracity, but the way a "true" story is remembered and retold can turn it into a false story very quickly.

Constructed False Memory

Two books would help non-believers to understand the effect of memory on storytelling and how the way ancient writers used to write their stories could turn them into false stories. One is *Memory: fragments of a modern history* by Alison Winter and the other is called *Forged: writing in the name of God: why the Bible's authors are not who we think they are* by Bart Ehrman.

Memory is a fascinating history of our understanding of how bad our human memories are; "terrible" would be a better adjective here. According to the researches done by the sources of the book, almost all of human memories are *constructed memories*.[3,4]

The literature on constructed false memory is extensive and worth focusing on. Non-believers need to know how false memories contribute to the emergence of new stories in human history. Also, non-believers need to know how false memories give the impression that a person could remember things that was supposed to be impossible to remember or to know.

An example of such false memories is when a person thinks he has received a message form a dead person as to inform him about the location of something in a dream, whereas he couldn't have possibly known such a fact without the dream. And then he takes that as the sign of a miracle. It usually turns out that the order of events are misremembered in such a way that the dream is taken as the messenger of the unknown rather than the other way around.

People usually come across information that their brains are too busy to fully attend to at the time, and then later they see the same information in a dream, thinking it was the dream that told them about that information. The order of events can easily reverse when they remember them. It can happen to anyone. Human brain is simply too easy to trick and memories are way too easy to fabricate. Impressions of this sort can make a person superstitious or make him believe in the unbelievable.

> "False memories may be full-blown memories of events that were never experienced or (perhaps more commonly) memories that are

> distorted (i.e., the event one is remembering actually occurred, but it did not occur in the way that is being recalled). Even though memory can foster an illusion of reliving an experience, it is actually a reconstruction and hence subject to departures from objective facts.
> [...]
> For example, when conveying anecdotes in casual social interactions, people sometimes embellish them to make them more interesting, often spicing them with fresh details in subsequent retellings to assure the desired pungency. Although innocent in intent, such embellishments can actually alter the teller's own memory of the event. Even though the raconteur might be fully aware of the fictional enhancements at the time, he or she may in time come to think of them as actual components of the original event [...]."[5]

This observation, that can be experimentally reproduced by anyone, makes us rely less on the veracity of testimonies that are usually the only building blocks of religious legends and myths. In cases where people did actually witness an event, their testimonies are unreliable (except for when there is a clear video of the event and the claims can be cross-referenced and corroborated) and can be distorted by suggestions.

The cases where no one actually was around when an alleged event occurred and people have nothing but anecdotes and hearsay stories that came presumably many years after the alleged event, the issue is even worse. Memory, in these cases, is less of an issue. One should suspect forgery.

The book *Forged* also touches upon the issue of memory, but it mainly focuses on humans' storytelling habits especially in ancient times. Not only people remember false stories, falsely remember true stories' chronologies, forget true stories in favour of fictions, and forget, but also they make up stories for many reasons. Ancient writers had many motives to forge stories, and they took full advantage of them. In *Forged* you can see it first-hand how early Christian writers made up stories and how we discovered these forgeries. Atheists would hugely benefit from this knowledge and would gain a good grip on the roles that ancient writers played in today's myths and fictions in Christianity.[24]

Again, you can see that we should not blame the victim because they have faulty memories or read forged stories. We all have faulty memories, and we all believe in some fictitious stories as true. We need to realize that a lot of this is unintentional and not premeditated. Some people are more vulnerable to brain fictions than others though. We can blame our brains for this and many other faults of our species, but remember that we all share similar genes. For that, we should not be angry at others.

We need to understand ourselves and try to build upon that understanding rather than attacking innocent people because they are humans with all human faults that we all share alike. If anything, this should make us a lot more cautious in our conversations and much more charitable towards believers when they tell us a false story, remember a constructed false memory, or refer to a forged historical writing. The way to fix these is not confrontation but understanding, sympathy, patience, and dedication. It takes time to fix these errors in anyone's thinking and nonbelievers cannot reasonably expect to be able to achieve any effective enlightenment over a half-an-hour heated conversation. Usually, it will not happen that way.

Confirmation bias

> "THE MISCONCEPTION: Your opinions are the result of years of rational, objective analysis.
> THE TRUTH: Your opinions are the result of years of paying attention to information that confirmed what you believed, while ignoring information that challenged your preconceived notions."[45]

As an omnipresent phenomenon, confirmation bias can be both a blessing and a curse. It is actually serving an important function in the mental life of every human as well as most other animals with brains. An animal brain filters out what it considers as noise and only picks up what it is interested in or has a reason to be interested in. This "ability" of the brain, if we call it so for evolutionary reasons, actually helps the limited resources of the brain to be allocated to a limited number of prioritized items instead of it being flooded by every relevant and irrelevant piece of information from the world. Our brains are not powerful enough to compute every bit of information that it receives from the peripheral neurons. It simply does not have the resources necessary to attend to all data it gets. There has to be ways for it to sieve out what is instrumental to its objectives from everything else. This instrumentalism of the brain causes what we know as confirmation bias. It is not all that bad or useless then.

It becomes annoying, however, when it gets on the way of intentional attempts to increase the accuracy of our perceptions. David McRaney describes it this way: "Confirmation bias is a filter through which you see a reality that matches your expectations. It causes you to think selectively, but the real trouble begins when confirmation bias distorts your active pursuit of facts."[45]

Like denial and cognitive dissonance that I talked about above, confirmation bias applies to both believers and non-believers. Here, what I am interested in is to raise awareness to the both sides of a Socratic dialogue regarding this serious issue.

Atheists do have as many confirmation biases as any other member of a society; no fewer, no more. The fact that many conversations between atheists and believers end up in having a bitter taste in the mouth of them both, shows that both sides are not able to properly see the reality of the state of affairs as they potentially should.

They both keep missing crucial facts about one another constantly and regularly. They both underestimate the intelligence of the other side. They both have the tendency of mixing up facts with statements and the state of affairs with our statements about the state of affairs (one cannot be true or false and the other can, because truth and falsity are *only* the properties of some sentences and are not applicable to emotions or state of affairs). They both underestimate the number of times each one utters totally nonsensical, false, or flatly stupid sentences. They exaggerate how smart they are and how dumb their opponents are. And they both take it for granted that what they think they know is actually what the fact of the matter is.

Most of these estimations, exaggeration, generalizations, and approximations that either side makes is actually fallacious, one way or another, and cannot be supported by enough evidence. This causes two major issues. One on each side of the fence.

On the atheists' side, they will form a distorted and usually wrong view about believers even if they used to be believers themselves. They start to think that they were different, those differences were substantial, and due to those differences they are now seeing the world as it actually is.

The question is not if there were differences, but how much difference were there and how significant were they? When we get closer to the issue, we usually find out that they probably were not as important as we want to think they were. Most of them were probably accidental and many of them were out of our control anyway. In this world, no one really deserves the accidental advantages they might find themselves having over anyone else. Nevertheless, most people do brag about them. They also do blame those who are less advantaged. This distortion of the views already sets the stage for a secret humiliation of whoever does not get it. It effectively cripples genuine engagements in conversations.

The emotional facet of atheists' talks are usually defective and distorted. They look down on the believers with whom they hold conversations. This unintentional condescension poisons the atmosphere from the get go. They got the factual side right, but they usually fail to communicate it properly and effectively due to their own confirmation biases. They unwittingly, and in most cases unintentionally, fail to see the whole picture that includes the emotional factors and the problems that their own biases are causing in a typical conversation.

The believers' side is not any better. Not only they carry all the biases that the atheists carry, they also carry more troubles than their non-believer friends. They have reality-checking problems on the top of all what I said about atheists.

Not only that they have the same biases as the atheists have regarding how poorly they judge them, but also they also think they "know" lots of "stuff" that are simply false. Without any exception, they all have deficiencies in their epistemology.

Confirmation bias is basically an epistemological problem. To learn how to avoid the epistemological pitfalls that have been plaguing almost every conversation between believers and non-believers that I have come across, one needs to work on one's skills in epistemology and logic.

One way to do that, of course, is to take university or college courses on those topics. There are many online courses available too with great quality and made by some of the best universities around the world. There are also university-level courses that one can buy from online bookstores or rent from libraries that are usually made by the best and the brightest educators on the planet. The prices of these courses, either university ones or the ones you can buy, are pretty much the same. Many of the freely-available online courses are also well worth the time and effort of taking and going through because many well-known universities, such as MIT, are behind them.

The other choice, which is not any less effective but is a bit less formal, is to read books. I am going to introduce two of the many available ones here.

My first pick is *A Manual for Creating Atheists* by Peter G Boghossian. This book is almost entirely dedicated to the epistemology of dialogues between believers and non-believers. Although it is not written as a textbook, it very well works as one. Unlike boring text-books, this is written for ordinary people like you and I. The tone is not formal, but it is not void of well-formed instructions on technical issues either. There are many valuable examples of scenarios in which you might find yourself at any time. Strategies to properly explain difficult concept and demonstrate how to reason well are proposed and discussed.

The second book that I am going to recommend is *Proving history: Bayes's theorem and the quest for the historical Jesus* by Richard Carrier. Although the title says that the book is about the historicity of Jesus, it does not actually talk about Jesus much. The book is written to lay the logical foundations for investigating stories that people tell, like the stories about historical figures, Jesus amongst them.[46]

The book employs a more technical approach and has some simple mathematics; nothing to hinder a highschool graduate from understanding the concepts.

This book addresses the induction reasoning issues that I discussed before. It demonstrates and proves that all inductive arguments, which we use in science, are Bayesian arguments; anything that depends on evidence. Then it explains, in details, how Bayesian arguments work. The techniques are fully applicable to all historical claims and I encourage any non-believer who wishes to discuss historical claims with anyone to read and to try to understand this unique book.

To generally understand the mistakes everyone makes in their reasoning, there are many great books of which these two are mention-worthy. (1)*You Are Not So Smart: Why You Have Too Many Friends on Facebook, Why Your Memory Is Mostly Fiction, and 46 Other Ways You're Deluding Yourself* and (2)*You Are Now Less Dumb: How to Conquer Mob Mentality, How to Buy Happiness, and All the Other Ways to Outsmart Yourself* both written by David McRaney. Although these books are not as technical as the two books I mentioned before, due to the numerous examples of daily logical mistakes that we all might make, it can give you a firm understanding of the self-deceptions and the illusions we all might be living with. This would put our own world-view into perspective, would humble the reader, and would help them sympathize a lot more with the rest of the people of the world. So they would realize that we all are not as smart as we might want to believe.[45,47]

Good intention

> The road to hell is paved with good intentions.
> — Anonymous

Ironic, eh?

Keep in mind that many believers have good intentions. As an ex-believer put it:

> "I wanted to be good. I wanted to be the best. I wanted to do the best possible. I wanted to know everything that there was to know to defend my religion. I didn't want to stutter, umm, or uhhh when someone was questioning my faith. I wanted to be ready to answer them and crush their arguments with my "evidence" and undeniable "reasons." I didn't want to be like the rest of the world, but to transcend them all in virtues and my readiness to defend what I used to believe. In that period of my life, had I come across you [the author of this book], I would have found you if I could and have taught you a lesson you wouldn't forget; because, you had insulted my faith. I could be serious about that, Eric."
> — An ex-believer friend

I can understand that point of view because I can relate to it. When I was a child and didn't know any better, I used to think that there might be "an invisible guy" in the sky or rather in my room who would have listened to me and could have possibly reacted to my communications. I was never fully convinced that it was so, because I tried to have a meaningful communication with the supposed entity and I failed every time. This was a clear sign to me that there was something terribly wrong with the whole idea. Nevertheless, I persisted in my trials and errors. I experimented a lot, took notes, real physical notes, about the details of my experiments and tried to find a pattern. Each and every time I, sort of, saw a pattern, I couldn't rule out many other explanations that could have been the possible reason why the pattern was perceived. The other explanations were irrevocably simple and terribly more plausible and effective than any supernatural explanation to me. However, I was a stubborn boy. I could not quit just yet.

I was not a particularly smart individual who could get it all at age two, like many atheists suspiciously claim, so it took me years of trial and error to finally come to the conclusion that it is all a sham.

My attention to supernaturals started at age 15 (before that I was not thinking about anything supernatural whatsoever). By the time I finished my high-school, I was almost certain that no answer will ever come from "the other side," and when I was halfway through my undergraduate school, every single argument and "evidence" in favour of supernatural had already fallen apart in my mind. The supernatural hypothesis could not withstand the monumental weight of the evidence I personally collected or come across in books and articles as an avid reader.

Nonetheless, before the entire hypothesis evaporated in my mind and left me with pure, elegant, and majestic reality, although not a believer in the strict sense of the term, I could easily relate to any of them. I was living amongst them, drinking with them, playing with them, being force-fed by their propaganda day in, day out, studying their crap in school and passing tests and exams on them, being forced to participate in common prayers, and trying to find ways to get around that with my other conspirators in school. When you live and breath such propaganda, you tend to absorb some of it as a little child after a while. Believers were all around me for at least 25 years of my life. I know them when I see one, and I can tell you exactly how they feel (at least most of them). They want to stand right before their imaginary friend. Many of them badly want that and try hard, constantly, and regularly to achieve that self-imposed objective; every day.

Non-believers can forget this once they have passed the point of no return for a few years. They can start to believe that they had always thought this way, that they had always been free from all form of superstitions. This constructed narrative can gradually become the memory of their self (remember false memories?) and they start to believe it as a fact. This is an innocent mistake. We all tend to forget traumatic, mental injuries, and let them go. So much so that we sometime even act as if they never happened. Therefore, those nonbelievers who used to believe, can fall into the false memory trap themselves and be too proud of themselves for the memory they constructed of their imagined self that had never been gullible enough to believe in any religion.

To those nonbelievers who never believed in the unbelievable to begin with, this might be the only natural state of affairs that they know of. If so, then everyone else looks and sounds abnormal to them.

This is also problematic. It reduces sympathy and understanding between the two groups and contributes to the emergence of similar in-group/out-group mentality of which they usually accuse believers. They are the pure kind after all, right? They have never been tainted with this nonsense, they might think. Then they would probably act upon that perception of self, even unintentionally. They should remember that it was as accidental for them to be born in the situation they ended up with as to be born in a fundamentalist family with a strong religious diet. They never had to repel absurdities as much as you and I had to, to be where we are after years of work. That is not a bad thing, but nothing to be proud of either. It is not much different from being proud of being tall or having a shoe size of 13. It is okay to wear shoes that are 13, but please don't brag about it and don't assume you deserve anything special because of that.

We all want to be better people. Some religious people are actually obsessed by this theme, or demand it if you wish. This is what is on their minds when they wake up in the morning, and what is on their minds when they go to bed at night. So, my ex-believer friend insisted that, they need help. They deserve help. They "deserve" it. "Deserve" means, "To acquire or earn a rightful claim, by virtue of actions or qualities, to (something); to become entitled to or worthy of (reward or punishment, esteem or disesteem, position, designation, or any specified treatment)."[48] Almost all humans share that specific "treatment" that these people deserve. We all deserve to be informed.

Believers are not necessarily believers because they want to be stupid. In many cases they are misinformed. Misinformation and deceit is everywhere in the air: the book they usually read, the place of worship they frequent, the "good news" they hear from most people around them, the Santa that brings them gifts, and most other aspects of their lives. It is a saturated life. Saturated in lies, fabricated stories, forgeries, "proofs," "evidence," and almost everything they read. They don't deserve this. No one deserves to live in a life saturated by lies. You, my dear atheist, have the duty to help, not to ridicule the unfortunate.

We also have to keep helping regularly and repeatedly. If you think of the extent of lies most believers are swimming in every day of their lives, you will agree that the mess in their minds cannot be cleaned up in one go, over a short comment exchanged on a forum, or after a conversation on a bus. If you think of religious people as friends and family members who need extended attention to get better at thinking, you would be a lot more patient before them. You would give them time to get better gradually. You would sympathise when they make mistakes, again. You would know that they are trying to be better people most of the time even if they never say so or never show the signs. You would know that you can never *make* them better people, but you are working *with* them to *enable* them to be better people; to share better tools with them, to show them how *they* can evaluate claims.

Christmas Bundle: Buy 1, get 4 free

When people are hit by any of them, the other four usually come for the ride too, and for the price of one. The most serious of the items in this list is 'loss and grief'. Then the other four are fear, hope, meaning, and self-deception. One's vulnerability to one of these items, also makes them a bit more prone to the others; it makes the others easier to appear and to stick around. Let us go through the list one by one and see what might happen when they strike an individual.

Loss and grief

We already know from the studies in cognitive science and psychology that when a person incurs a great loss, be it financial, emotional, or otherwise, they become almost immediately emotionally unstable and fragile. If the loss is irreparable, like losing a beloved family member or a friend, then the emotional injury heightens to the extent that it may take days, week, or even months and years before the wounds are finally healed. Sometimes the healing is never complete and the emotional scars remain all over a person's psyche.

As if this is not bad already, these traumatic experiences usually destabilize a person's self-esteem, and weaken their rationality and logic. The person becomes a lot more open to suggestions, no matter how obscure they might be, and becomes less critical of their merits because of the lowered self-esteem and the less trust that the person put on their own sound judgement.

Imagine a person who used to think of himself as happy and healthy, suddenly gets a news: 'You only have one more year to live. You have a rare type of brain cancer. You are doomed in a year or so.' Assuming that this is an ordinary person with ordinary plans and hopes, their life suddenly turns upside-down. "Traumatic!" one can call this sudden revelation. The first reaction to this in most people is that they panic, deny, become anxious, and start searching for possible fixes whatever the cost might be.

The self-esteem is already wounded. One used to think of oneself as invincible. "I was alright a week ago, and now I am diagnosed with cancer! It must be wrong! There has to be a way out of this." When possible cures are ruled out one by one, the desperation starts to set in. The feeling that something, somewhere, somehow, and someday must be available to cure me. Only if I could find it.

This is exactly the point at which most ordinary people might try weird alternative medicine practices and believe in any claim that gives them any impossible-sounding promise. At this stage, nothing sounds too impossible to them, and since they are going to die anyway, it won't hurt to try this homoeopathic remedy or that spell, or prayer. "What about energy therapy? Yeah! Let's try that too. What if it works? There are a lot of things in this world that we know nothing about, right? Then homoeopathy might be one of them? How do you know if it is not?" And this can be a slippery slope that leads them to accept even more weird things.

When someone loses a family member, a lover, a father, a mother, or any significant person in their lives, they also become as irrational as one can get at times. It depends on the person's background beliefs and the perceived severity of the loss. Catastrophic losses can make one's world view collapse altogether. They become easy prey to opportunistic memes and belief systems. The most vulnerable time in anyone's life is usually sitting at these conjunctions.

Religions, all of them, bet heavily and take full advantage of these. They have a ready solution to all of one's problems. *All* of them!

Hope

Once emotionally destabilized, a person can be more easily persuaded to believe in the unbelievable. If the burning desire to survive a terrible accident or disease, desire to see a deceased, loved one, or a desire to fix a terrible catastrophe gets too pressing, and if the environment is contaminated enough with religious "solutions," then the time is ripe to harvest the fruits of the mixture. All religions have perfect, albeit usually fully incompatible and opposing, absolute solutions to all imaginable problems. "Did your mother pass away? Do you want to see her? Here you go!

Buy this package and you will see her again," and the package is usually filled with the most absurd assumptions, claims, and promises conceivable.

> "*The Architect* : Humph. Hope, it is the quintessential human delusion, simultaneously the source of your greatest strength, and your greatest weakness."[49]

The hope to see a deceased person, the hope to survive an accident, the hope that a homoeopathic remedy might actually work, and the hope that praying can bring back a parted husband from dead, can make people do the weirdest things.

> "A woman left her husband's body rotting in a bedroom of their home because she thought he would rise from the dead, a Hamilton court heard Monday. [...] [She] slept in the bed with her husband for one night, just before he died. Then she noticed his stomach was bloating and rigor mortis was setting in on his forehead, court documents show. "We were trusting God ... we thought, 'OK Lord, you know better,'" [she] told the Spectator. "[She] and her five children who resided in the house are devout Christians and thought [he] would be resurrected and therefore kept the door locked and waited for him to come to life," Booy wrote. "There were also friends who resided at the house. They all prayed on a daily basis for Peter to come back to life.""[50]

As simple as it is to ridicule her, and it is a patently ridiculous thing that must enter the *Guinness Book of World Records* for gullibility, it is, at the same time, an example of misplaced hopes, personal love, and desire to reverse and fix reality. I bet no serious charges would be laid against her aside from health issues it might have caused to the public. And I agree with such a verdict too.

I think she and her family are in need of serious mental help rather than punishment. When the distortion of reality reached this point, the person cannot legitimately be held responsible for what she has done. Do you really believe a person whose judgement has been incapacitated to this extent is blameworthy of what she has done? Her family and the other "residents" in that household seem to be as mentally ill as the wife herself.

When I say religious beliefs are insane and can make people do insane deeds, I don't mean we should start blaming the victims. It is religion that makes people attempt such absurdities, but it is the desperation and hope that make them chose these options out of others. The religions must be blamed, not the religious in this case. The believer is simply an ill person that needs to be mentally treated. She needs help.

I doubt you would ever hear non-believers do things like this. Of course there can be insane non-believers and sick non-believers and psychopath non-believers like in any other human population. That is not my point. My point is that any type of mental and physical illness must be professionally treated and the victims of these illnesses should be seen as patients, not criminals with full mental capacities expected of an adult human being.

When engaging in conversations with believers, we need to always remind ourselves of these possibilities. That the one we are talking to might have lost a dear person and sincerely hope to see that person again somehow. They might not care about how. They care only about if. And religion always gives them false hope. If they are in the state of denial, then it would be nearly impossible to make them see reality as it actually is. 'Reality as is' would not cut it for them. It is not enough. And if things can get right only through magic, then that is what they want and wish to be true. If it takes incredible things to happen so that they can be reunited with their beloved ones, they are not bothered. As long as the label on the bottle says: "Drink me!" they would do just that. What is in the bottle is not their concern.

Also, when people are desperate and need serious help, they won't accept non-believer's claim that, let's say, acupuncture won't work and homoeopathy is quackery. They cannot even hear you. The only thing they can hear in their heads is, "What if it works? Trying it is not going to hurt anyway." That's all they hear and that is all they want to hear. So, non-believers must understand where the desperate, the grieving, and the hopeful are coming from. So they can patiently work within their frame of reference to gradually make them correct their misconceptions.

Only an extended period of attention and hard work, cooperation, social/emotional support, and intellectual education might stand a chance of dispelling the deeply rooted myths and false beliefs.

Atheists who do not take these into account and instead try to attack believers as if they are clinging to only one stupid idea that can be corrected quickly and painlessly, only making fools of themselves. Not only more than one or even one set of errors are involved in one's broken, religious belief system, but also a huge amount of emotions, hopes, expectations, and sorrows are playing constant roles.

Atheists can very easily address those former intellectual items as they usually do. What they almost invariably neglect is the emotional elements. Although atheists cannot substitute the religion's lies with another set of lies just to fix the problems of believers, they can enable them to successfully substitute reality for lies and gradually build up a richer repository of facts to work with to go about their day to day lives.

Education is the central missing piece in this puzzle. When people have no idea about the bigger macro-cosmos of the universe and the micro-cosmos of the biological machines, they commit more mistakes than they would have, had they been intimately acquainted with them.

Religious biologists and physicists can also be found. So, learning those subjects is not sufficient to make a person able to tell myths from realities. Also, the emotional part of human reasoning is still there, regardless of the subject one might take in a college. Nevertheless, not knowing these subjects is a shortcut to the acquisition of superstitions and religious lies. Modern physics and biology are strong antidotes to cure ignorance out of which most religious beliefs spring.

Meaning

> ""People want to escape suffering, but if they can't get out of it, they want to find meaning," Norenzayan says. "For some reason, religion seems to give meaning to suffering–much more so than any secular ideal or belief that we know of.""[51]

When people find solace in hoping that they will eventually reunite with the love of their life, albeit in the life after, or when they sincerely hope that quackery would help them survive, then these beliefs give meanings to their lives. Facing a great desperation, when they hear that they will sit on the right side of the king of the world beyond the grave, or when they are told that all of their miseries will end once they enter the kingdom of god(s), or if they kill infidels, it will surely reserve them a spot in heaven with seventy-two virgins running up and down their poles, then they feel even their misery has a purpose, a meaning, and is not all in vain.

Whether it is trading your current life to gain a place in the kingdom of Zeus in the life after, or it is to just make you feel less miserable in return for your unquestioned loyalty, religions have you covered. The emotional benefits one would gain from selling one's mental freedom to a religious belief system overwhelms all the intellectual gains that the person would gain by knowing the truth. This wishful thinking always has negative effects on all societies. The temporary band-aids that religions put on people's problems make them happy enough for the moment. And since humans, by nature, are not known to be the animal with the best foresights, they always miss the larger picture and lose anyway at the end. But, many people won't care. Because by the time the shit hits the fan, they are already dead for quite a while. They cannot care by then. The society as a whole is what has to pay for the gullibilities of its individuals and everyone would be screwed indirectly. As long as it is an indirect cost, no one cares.

Religions offer pre-made and ready-to-consume packages of meaning to masses. You just need to subscribe to them and give them the key to your mind and pocket. That's all. The price does not seem that big and at times it can be almost invisible and intangible.

On the opposite side, non-believers don't have any ready meals on offer. "You have to find your own meaning in life" or "I cannot tell you what the meaning of life is. It can be anything to anyone. What is it to you? You have to search and find it for yourself," are usually the best advice atheists have to offer in this department. I bet it is way less appealing an offer than seventy-two virgins in heavens to any man (I bet there are similar deals for women in a segregated part of the heaven).

You cannot beat that. I am sorry, but nothing that atheists might ever say can ever sound as good as an imaginary heaven. And because it is an imaginary product and service, it is cheap to build, to develop, and to make incredible. It can incorporate even magic and things that are impossible in reality. How can you beat that with anything real? Reality is incredible, awesome, and all that, but so far as human needs and hopes are concerned, reality is not designed to accommodate us. It is the other way around. We have evolved to take the most possible advantage out of what is available. The same reality can change overnight, and we turn into ashes. The end of the story. Huh! And you want to compete with heavens that are specially tailored, in believers' minds though, to cater to all the wildest desires of humans? Even the ones that they are not wild enough to conceive of but they will love once they taste? Good luck with that!

I cannot emphasise enough on the enormity of this disparity and the problems it causes in the way of disillusioning believers. Your task is effectively this: You want to convince a person that (1) Their reassurance of the promised land with all the goodies, wild sex, and wine (and perhaps cocaine, you never know) is nothing but illusionary wishful thinking, (2) They are gullible to believe such a nonsense (3) the situation they are living in, which can be miserable or deficient in many ways, is what is real, and (4) there is nothing else but this very reality and nowhere else beyond the graves.

As you can see, the stacks are piled against the non-believer and the task is monumental. If anything, the chances are that nothing can move that mountain, ever.

The highly toxic and addictive cocktail of religion cannot be taken away from a believer to leave them with a vacuum in their heart and mind. If you don't have anything to fill in the vacuum with, you are doomed to fail. Addiction to drugs follows a similar pattern. One cannot take away the addiction of a drug-addict by merely talking to them. It is not going to happen.

In the face of this observation, what do you think that letting go of the cozy illusions can offer a believer to change her behaviour and to make them a better, more rational, and much more emotionally healthy person?

If the meaning of life is not to go to heaven and spend the eternity in a whore house, then what is it?

If we will die and everything that is happening ends in nothing beyond the graves, then why should we bother? What does it all mean then?

It won't help to remind the believer that things do not have meanings. Knowing that although life doesn't have any meaning—rather than what we might give to it—we can all seek happiness, harmony, beauty, and love just as easily, might not console a believer right away. "How?" they might ask. Even if you tell them, "You ate an ice cream yesterday. How was it? You loved listening to that music the other night. How did that feel? You felt warmth and your heart was filled with love when you bought a pair of shoes for that homeless person on Broadway. How did that feel? All the meanings, feelings, and emotions are going to be there, albeit towards much healthier subjects," they still resist. For some weird reason they want to believe that the kind of meaning *they* talk about is, somehow different from everything you mentioned, but they cannot quite tell you how.

This is due to the long-lasting effects of the brainwashing that all religions give all of their victims. They convinced them that the kind of half-hearted and totally-conditional love that their cult offers, which is almost universally tribal and only applies to the in-groups, is qualitatively different from the love that the secular world experiences. They are lead to believe that they have something superior. Ask them how it is superior to the love you talked about, and then you will see their perplexity. They cannot give you any answer that, at best, is any different in quality than the secular, universal love. Still, they believe that they are talking about "something else."

They are convinced that it is the invisible guy in the sky that is the source of meaning in their lives and that he can never be substituted, replaced, or simply discarded.

Religions convince the believers that what *they* say and recommend being exercised is the only way that things must and can be done. They never advertise against themselves and tell the truth. They never say that more often than not, not only religions do not make things any better, but also complicate relationships, damage trust, condition people to commit insane acts, and are the worst choices that can be made in today's world. What kind of advertising would that be otherwise.

We are all atheists in regard to the religions we do not practice and that is alright. We do not fall up to the sky because we do not believe in Poseidon. We do not lose all purpose and meaning in our lives because we never thought of Ra or don't give a darn what Cronus might think of us in this life. For all practical purposes, there is no Poseidon, Ra, or Cronus for most of us to begin with. We cannot care less about them in general. And all of this is fine with us. Then why can't we extend this feeling of fineness to the last deity on our list? Suddenly all the meanings disappear from our lives if Allah, Vishnu, Lord, or Yahweh is discarded? Isn't it weird?

You can see how groundless the sense of security and the source of meaning in believers' minds are. It is the simplest observation that a four-years child can successfully complete, and yet, most adults are so badly brainwashed that their capacity to comprehend such a simple observation is substantially diminished. How distorted one's rationality must be in order not to see the simple comparison I made above? And yet, there are billions of believers of all sort of myths on this planet.

The unparalleled power of the organized religion to brainwash shines through. The fact that so many people are so badly infected only tells us the extent of the propaganda. Billions of dollars are spent every year to keep up these lies and myths and refresh the minds of the followers with more of the less.

Religion offers them meaning. The challenge is how to dismantle their numerous, false claims and how to console humans with reality.

Atheists need to gather their wits and compile information and guidances. They need to write more clearly about the ways a secular life have meaning. We need to explain how you and I keep living a happy and enriched life without illusions and wishful-thinking and how no illusion is needed for a fulfilled life. It needs to be explained what a person can do to give meaning and purpose to one's life without appealing to the myths and expired illusions that religions perpetuate. It might sound funny, but you need to create step-by-step pamphlets and guidebooks. Some people cannot figure it out by themselves. They need help and the responsibility is on the shoulders of the secular world to come up with rational guides and maps.

How to do it? I don't know, but don't waste people's time if you don't have any handy. Stay out of serious conversations if you cannot back up your plans, and if you don't have any alternative plan to begin with. Stay quiet if you cannot explain "how," because the chances are that you might not know it yourself. Don't confuse your believer friends with generic, useless clichés such as "find the meaning for yourself" because if they could, they would not have been in this poor, intellectual condition in the first place. They are where they are, usually, because they cannot think for themselves. Don't confuse them if you are not helping either. Leave them alone or find someone who has the right tools to deal with the situation effectively and properly.

Remember that if you are not a dentist, you don't have to pull out people's rotten teeth. Leave it to the experts and those who know how. Otherwise, you will cause more troubles than you might solve.

The Good Book — A Humanist Bible by Grayling is a step in the right direction.

> "Drawn from the wealth of secular literature and philosophy in both Western and Eastern traditions, using the same techniques of editing, redaction, and adaptation that produced the holy books of the Judeo-Christian and Islamic religions, *The Good Book* consciously takes its design and presentation from the Bible. In its beauty of language and its arrangement into short chapters and verses for ease of reading and quotability, it offers the non-religious seeker all the wisdom, insight, solace, inspiration, and perspective of secular

> humanist traditions that are older, far richer, and more various than Christianity. Organized in twelve main sections-Genesis, Histories, Wisdom, The Sages, Parables, Consolations, Lamentations, Proverbs, Songs, Epistles, Acts, and the Good-*The Good Book* opens with meditations on the origin and progress of the world and human life in it, then devotes attention to the question of how life should be lived, how we relate to one another, and how vicissitudes are to be faced and joys appreciated. [...]"[52]

You don't have to be a non-believer to enjoy the wealth of wisdom that is presented in this book, which is a great advantage. The book is not written to advocate atheism *per se*, nor is it *about* atheism. It poses as a blueprint for a happy human life filled with the wisdom of ages. As such, both believers and non-believers hugely benefit from reading this book, will find solace in its wise advice, as well as lots of instructions as to how handle life's challenges (and death too). Anyone with any religious orientation or with no religious inclinations can learn a lot from it as this is a collection "[i]nspired by the writing of Herodotus and Lucretius, Confucius and Mencius, Seneca and Cicero, Montaigne, Bacon, and so many others [...]."[52]

This book is a great start. We need many more books like this with less obvious—and hence less sensitizing—intentions.

Fear

The beast non-believers are facing is not the poor believer who is trying to have a friendly conversation with others on a religious forum. He or she is a reflection of us. In many ways, humans are all the same. The believer would not have come forth to engage in a dialogue if she meant harm. You as a non-believer are talking with a person who is frustrated in many ways, either thinking that you and your friends are rubbing the world of its meanings, or even risk the possibility of being burnt in hell for eternity. They do not want that to happen. They might genuinely care for people or be scared for your life after death.

If the only alternative to burning in an eternal, fierce fire in an afterworld (and usually losing your head in this world), is to utter a long spell five times a day with your head touching the ground while your bum is hanging up in the air, many people, if not most, would go for the latter option.

If you are a believer reading this book, I am not sure if you ever have to chose between those two, but if you had, I am willing to bet that your bum is hanging up in the air right now, or will be in a short while.

If you are a Muslim, you already "know" that if you become a non-believer, then Allah will throw you in a physical hell and use you as a cheap supply of log for its eternal hell-fire. Each time that your skin burns away, he grows a new one for you to feel the pain again, and he does this *forever*. Forever, you know?

'Forever' is a long time, just in case you didn't realize. The torture never ends and you will never get any relief. If this was what you genuinely believed, what would you have done?

Although all believers might not believe in such punishments, many of them do. Out of those who do, many believe in it firmly and take it very seriously. The seriousness and the reality of that image is strong enough in their minds that motivate them to act upon the conviction.

Imagine that I suddenly tell you that all the stories you have heard about jails and the related documents, films, documentaries, as well as everything people say about them are fake, fabricated, lies, false, and non-existent. There is no jail whatsoever. We would still pay the price of our wrongdoings in other ways but there is no legal system to take care of all of these. There has never been. Everything you have read, seen on a TV, and are told about jails have always been completely made-up stories. What would you say? Are you convinced?

If you said no, i.e. if you were not convinced, even if you had never seen any of them first-hand, you are in a perfect position to understand what some believers might think and feel when you tell them that there is no hell and no afterlife. It just sounds like nonsense to them. You sound like a nut-case to them and for good reasons.

They cannot believe what you just told them in the same way you could not believe my claims about jails. Although, I hope you probably have never been in any of them, you still could not believe my claim that they didn't exist. Believers are the same. They feel almost exactly the same when you ask them to discard their false beliefs.

Why is that? Assuming that you haven't been in a jail in your life, why do you think that they exist? What are your reasons? "It just makes sense," you might say. "It fits the puzzle and if you put all the pieces and the evidence for it together, how the society works, how people do their things, what you are sure about and what you are reassured about by others, all point to one thing: That jails do exist.

Have you watched *The Truman Show* or *Westworld*? (Spoiler alert! If you haven't watched them yet, you might want to skip the next few sentences.) How do you know that the entire world around you is not fabricated to make it look real while it's merely a show or a game for others to enjoy? How do you know that everything you are taught in school is not tampered with to perpetuate a lie?[53] "It would be very hard to keep such an enormous conspiracy from leaking out. I would have known it by now," you might say.

How about *The Matrix*? (Spoiler alert) How do you know we all are not living in a simulated world?[54] There won't be any indication that we can use to tell a simulated world apart from a real world, because our simulated world could be designed to make all the would-be-clues unimportant or even counterintuitive, so we won't take them seriously. Then any seam would look totally fine to us, simulated beings, in such a world by design. How do you know if that is not the case right now?

The funny thing is that not only you don't know the answer to this later question, but also you cannot know it. It is a self-referential world and there is no logical way to get out of such a world by the means available inside of the world. You can try though.

If you got a weird feeling by now regarding questioning the most obvious things that you might ever believe in, then you know very well how real and obvious some religious threats might be to some believers. It is *real* to them—like a hell!

Because they feel its reality, and they live in the shadow of its imminent threats, you as a non-believer cannot legitimately reject their fears and tell them they are insane for believing in such myths. It will never work in those cases. If the fears are instilled into their psyche from childhood, as it is the case with the practices of many religions such as Christianity and Islam, then it is almost hard-coded like their mother tongue. Can you make anyone forget their mother tongue? If you know the answer to this question, then you also have an idea how possible it might be to dismantle the fear of hell in the mind of an adult who has been threatened by it from day one.

And yet, fear of eternal punishment is not the only fear that makes minds more religious. There are all sorts of other fears.

Unfortunately, the consensus amongst experts is that as life gets tough, the tendency to be more vulnerable to superstition goes up.[51] That means, at the time of difficulties, people start to go back to the only comforting corner they used to know. You can see this tendency after each big hurricane, tsunami, earthquake, terrorist attacks, or other catastrophe. People start to pray even if they used not to. People start to go to churches even when they had never done so. Look at a footage of a real hostage situation in a public place and look at the faces of the hostages. Many of them even show their religious thoughts through their body language. One might draw crosses on their chest. Another might hold their hands for prayer. Yet another person might kiss the cross that is hanging from their necklace. This sign is so prevalent that is used, almost exactly as I mentioned above, in films for the effects they induce: They imply that the person who is doing so is shitting their pants; that's how scared they are.

Therefore, fear is a catalyst for the return of religiosity and religious behaviours.

How should atheists approach this dilemma? That's a good question!

I don't know how. We need to study the field a lot more before we can issue a verdict. Most fears can be dealt with through direct, intentional and assisted confrontations. But, has it been that easy, most phobias would have disappeared by now.

Any technique that would be effective at letting an individual go of a phobia, might become instrumental in freeing minds in this department too. Specially the studies of Merel Kindt on the subject of phobia seems extremely promising.[55-59]

I imagine that encouragements, positive reinforcements, assisted confrontation, and a lot of emotional back-up would be on the list of tools that we might need to fight this complexity. I am sure we will discover many more techniques when we properly study the matter.

Self-deception

Do you remember the main title of this section? It was "Christmas Bundle: buy 1, get 4 for free." When you buy into a religious mentality because of a loss, an unfulfilled hope, searching for a meaning or a purpose, or because of fear, then the other elements of the religion you happened to come across will eventually squeeze themselves into your mentality. They all come as a bundle. Once one came in, the others will follow.

However, the question is how a smart, educated person can really believe in strange myths as truth?

There are many well-written books and articles on 'why we believe what we believe', 'why we believe in weird or even false things', 'why rational people do stupid things and believe in irrational things',[60,61] and if we are 'born to believe' in weird myths.[6,62] Evolutionary biologists and social anthropologists have already unearthed the biological and social causes and mechanisms underlying our believing behaviours.

Evolutionary biologists are hard at work to discover how, precisely, we evolved to have the set of brain parts that make us believe in weird things. They have been telling us the story behind the evolutionary pressures that have driven our species to have the sort of brain that it has.

Social anthropologists have done a lot of grand works to compare the religious habits of different societies, the ancestors of the current societies, and the isolated populations of humans to see how they all are related. They discovered many similarities in their stories and myths, their habits, and beliefs. They have found patterns that repeat almost invariably throughout the lands as well as the ages. We are beginning to see the bigger picture of our species' religious habits.

These discoveries point to several elements that allow even the smartest of humans to believe in the weirdest ideas. One of them is self-deception.

"THE PHENOMENON

[M]uch controversy surrounds the effort to characterize the process of self-deception, the nature of the phenomenon itself, and the sort of irrationality characteristic of the phenomenon. Notwithstanding this disagreement, clear instances of what we call "self-deception" come readily to mind. The stock and shopworn example of the husband who, even though in possession of compelling evidence of his wife's infidelity, nonetheless insists upon her faithfulness is a case in point. Our husband may generate richly ornamented stories the apparent aim of which is to explain away the, by our lights, dispositive evidence of the fact of his wife's affairs. He may focus upon the occasions on which his wife has displayed great solicitousness and affection towards him, and he may well regard these data as clear and compelling evidence of her continued love for him. Moreover, he may subject evidence that strongly points towards his wife's infidelity to sustained and withering critical scrutiny, while precipitately embracing data indicative of her continued faithfulness. In short, our hapless husband repeatedly searches for reassuring evidence and probes various hypotheses in a sustained and continuing fashion in order to arrive at and then to retain the favored belief against various threats. Core cases of self-deception would, then, appear to involve a subject engaging in strategies the aim of which is the embrace of some proposition(s)."[63]

You might ask that since this applies to the circumstance where the self-deceiver knows the truth at some level, how is this going to apply to religion and religious beliefs? It has not been long ago that we had no idea how winds blow and how lightnings strike after all. We didn't know that gods didn't exist. We just discovered it now. How does self-deception apply to the ancient humans?

To address this concern I have to add that first of all, it is not news that there is no god(s) and all of these myths are, well, myths. At least since Democritus, many have already guessed that, with some qualifications that do not matter now, there are only atoms and void. At least our species had gone that far and the evidence were abundant enough to espouse such a hypothesis about 2400 years ago. So, no. It is not news.

Secondly, people who were making up those stories knew that they, themselves, made them up. However, they might have tended to forget it. But that does not matter. When a person makes up stories, that does not mean he "knows" that the events in the story actually happened. Quite the opposite. He knows, positively, that the stories were made up by himself.

When someone goes around and spreads false stories, as most shamans do to establish their own narrative of the way the universe works, then they knew they were not telling the truth.

What about the village inhabitants who actually believe in the forged stories by the elder shaman? Are they self-deceiving too?

The shaman is not self-deceiving by the way. He is deceiving others. He tells lies. Others who believe in what the shaman tells them can be true believers indeed. That means they might not self-deceive either. We all self-deceive at one point but this might not be one of them.

Given all these, it is not difficult to see that most villagers are being deceived and that could be all there to explain their religious behaviour. Also, we already know that many people of the old ages were illiterate and had no means to educate themselves; financially and intellectually deprived of what could have been available to a prince or a princess.[24] People couldn't learn. There were only a handful people in some cities who could read and even fewer who could write. Many could sign their names though, but that does not count as literacy. Therefore, we immediately see that deception had been a way more prevalent way for made-up stories to spread. People didn't have an easy time to educate themselves and become able to tell truth from lies (as if they can do so today). Still, our species had the means to, tentatively, arrive at the conclusion that there is nothing but atoms and void (Democritus). Self-deception becomes a bigger issue as we get closer to the modern age.

After the invention of movable types and press, the Bible became available to the common person. But, that was not the only book that became available. Soon after Gutenberg, all sorts of books started to be mass-produced. Therefore, buying books that used to be a luxury, not affordable to most people, became less of a burden.

Because of the Gutenberg's invention, the 15th century turned into a pivotal era in the human history.[64]

Fast-forward 300 years to the 18th century and to the time of Paul Heinrich Dietrich. His book, called *The System of Nature*, was one of the first attempts to aggregate the available arguments against any type and form of supernatural being. The arguments in his book are so rich and extensive that one is forced to believe that he could not possibly be the author of them all. They are just too many of them, and they are too diverse for one person to be able to think them all up alone. That's why it makes the reader think of the richness and the depth of the knowledge of humans at that time regarding the impossibility and the improbability of a supernatural being. The ideas seemed to be around for a long time.

Again, I am lead to believe that there had been plenty of ways for a common person to be disillusioned. I am talking about Europe at the end of the medieval period. Many other countries were in a sharp intellectual decline, or had just started their head-first dive to the prehistoric mentality of myths, ghouls, genies, and lamps (some of them have not reached the bottom of the pot yet. The prime examples of those nations are Iran (which is getting worse religiously while the rest of the world is getting better[51]), Afghanistan, Iraq, Saudi Arabia, and several others).

As we reach today's world, deception becomes the lesser player in the overall game and self-deception becomes the major actor of this game.

Although we can successfully argue that the prehistoric humans did not have the means to know better, we cannot excuse the modern people, as the ignorance seems to be a state chosen by many.

> "In the age of information, ignorance is a choice."
> — Donny Miller

In the 21st century, when you ask "How could he believe that?", self-deception usually comes on the top of the list of the reasons.

But how is self-deception possible? How can I know something and at the same time make myself believe that what I know is not true?

Here is the problem put in more technical terms:

> "The acquisition of a belief will make for self-deception only under the following conditions: A has evidence on the basis of which he believes that p is more apt to be true than its negation; the thought that p, or the thought that he ought rationally to believe that p,

motivates A to act in such a way as to cause himself to believe the negation of p. The action involved may be no more than an intentional turning away from the evidence in favor of p, or it may involve the active search for evidence against p. All that self-deception demands of the action is that the motive originate in a belief that p is true ... and that the action be performed with the intention of producing belief in the negation of p. Finally, and this is what makes self-deception a problem, the state that motivates the self-deception and the state it produces co-exist."[65]

How could they coexist? To explain this phenomenon, several mechanisms are suggested.[66,67] The details of the explanations are beyond the scope of this book. I recommend the reader to consult the bibliography at the end of this book for further readings. The reasons boil down to one point that humans are capable of holding contradictory beliefs, plus humans can commit very elaborate, mental gymnastics.

"[...] The self-deceiver might well, as Davidson suggests, intentionally turn his attention away from evidence supportive of the threatening belief and seek out evidence of the favored belief with the aim of inducing in himself the latter. But if this plan is to succeed, it is not easy to see how the self-deceiver could fail to be wholly taken in by his ruse. That is, a condition of success of such a project would appear to be that the conviction that he ought rationally to believe the epistemically sanctioned proposition be exiled or come to be regarded as epistemic[a]lly undermined before he can come to accept that his favored proposition is true. This is, however, very near to the sort of gambit recommended by Blaise Pascal in order to induce belief in the existence of God. There is no doubt that we can intentionally bring about conditions the result of which is that we come to believe what, at the time we brought about those conditions, we took ourselves to have no good reason to believe."[63]

How are atheists supposed to deal with this?

If the self-deception is pathological, as is alluded to in *Brain Fiction*[67], there is very little anyone can do to bring the 'patient' to their senses, unless the physiological issues that caused the symptoms are adequately addressed. This is obviously entirely out of the scope of any friendly conversation that we usually have with a believer. Today's science is not advanced enough to fix the underlying conditions that cause this category of issues yet. So, don't hold your breath for a solution to this problem, because it is not coming anytime soon.

The other self-imposed deceptions or, shall I call it self-imposed ignorance, is a lot easier to deal with, although it is still hard enough that gives any person nightmares and headaches.

People start to guess that something might be wrong with their world-view. They start to smell fishy things in the claims that their religions makes. Then they panic. They suddenly fear that they might be losing their faith. The solution to it? They shut their ears even harder. It is this category of people we need to patiently talk to and help let go of their fears.

Most religions have specially crafted techniques to fight back "doubt." They actually call it just that. "What to do when faced with doubt," and "How to defeat doubt," and titles like these. I have a pamphlet in which the instructions read under the following titles:

1. admit that you have sinned;
2. confess and repent;
3. forsake the sins of your past;
4. believe in Jesus Christ;
5. invite Jesus into your heart and life;
6. get a copy of God's Book, the Bible;
7. start talking to God;
8. seek Christian companions;
9. promise to continue to live for God;
10. tell others of your salvation; and
11. go to 1 and repeat.

It sounds pretty much like a modern computer algorithm. It reminds me of the BASIC programs I used to write when I was a child. A simple program in BASIC can go like this:

```
10 let i = 1
20 print i
30 i = i + 1
40 goto 20
```

This program has a problem though. It never ends! It prints the value of i, starting from 1, and keeps going. There is no condition written in the program to stop it. And that is a serious issue in any program.

The pamphlet seems to be suggesting exactly that. Also, pay close attention to items 6 to 10. These are reinforcing one's false beliefs by exposing the person to the same biased ideas over and over; to saturate the person's belief system with the dogma.

Most people do follow those instructions. Because they (1) are fearful of losing their faith and much more with it and (2) they believe that they are doing the right thing.

In many cases, the temptation of an eternal heaven and all what it might bring to the person is also a huge motivator. To them, it is never enough to live a finite life. They are certainly greedy so much so that they want an ever-lasting life with all the extras (if that is not greed, then what is it?)

They are also instructed to decisively abandon any non-believer friend or family members. This way, they are kept in the darkness of the dogma they are saturating themselves with. But who is keeping them there?

The decision must be made, eventually, by the person themselves, hence the self-deception.

So, when a person starts to sense that something is actually wrong with the nonsense they are fed with, there they go through the vaccination process, so they get back on line.

The self-deception part comes when they know that they sensed something was wrong and triy to suppress it. Although they cut their common sense off-line as soon as they could, the realization that they had such a cognition remains. They try to ignore it, because they "know" that if they allow it to flourish, it might take root and get harder to suppress. It also makes them anxious, because they believe that it is a seed of sin and the end result not only could cost them their ticket to heavens, but also can buy them a ticket to hell and an eternal punishment.

Those who believe in religions without heaven and hell, still have other worries. They want to stand right before their god(s), follow their god's commands, so they can have a perfect life, or many other reasons. Some might fear an immediate revenge of their chosen deity. Others might be more concerned about the reactions of the society in which they live. "What will happen if the doubt takes root and I lose my faith? What would everyone in the village would say? Are they going to burn me on the stake like my uncle who voiced his doubts?"

When the fear is strong, one can actually convince oneself to even forget something one once knew. If you have not watched or read *1984* by George Orwell, you owe it to yourself to do so as quickly as you can. It tells you what can be achieved if enough terror is induced in one's mind. The matter of self-deception is masterfully put into an unforgettable play.

Again, what can we do to deal with this situation?

As you have guessed by now, whatever the mechanism of self-deception might be, assuming that it actually occurs, it is tightly influenced and directed by denial, cognitive dissonance, emotional needs, false memories, confirmation biases, losses and griefs, hopes, meaning and purposes, and fears. As such, an effective strategy needs to be dynamically adjusted according to the cause or causes of the phenomenon. That is to say, there does not seem to exist any single fix or strategy to deal with this issue. If the 'fear' of death and its 'denial' is what has caused the terminally ill person to resort to irrational behaviour in the 'hope' that the death can be avoided somehow, then you need to deal with the fear, anxiety, denial, and hope as the instigators of the irrational beliefs. These elements are not the reasons the individual is infected by a religion. They exacerbate the infection. The reason the religion is invented and spread around could be a totally different story.

As a non-believer, you need to diagnose the complications that fan the flame of religiosity before you can devise any effective strategy to help a religious person. In many cases you would notice that the combination of fear, needs, hopes, and the other elements block your intervention from the get go. Being condescending to a patient would be adding insult to injury. Not only will it not work (even being sarcastic won't work), but also it makes the resistance of the individual in question deeper and harder to dismantle.

If that happens, the harm that might be caused to the individual could be bigger than any potential gain.

I have heard of arguments in favour of a kind of shock therapy, i.e. revealing the whole truth all at once so the audience finds itself in shock and disbelief; e.g. suddenly telling a child that "There is no Santa. It all was a lie and nothing more." I used to be persuaded by them for a very long time. I've even had several successes with that strategy. However, my failures have been way more numerous. I cannot justify or recommend this strategy any longer. Some would say that the shock would set the doubting machine in motion in the mind of a believer although they might initially show a reverse reaction and adamantly deny such a thing.[40] I am not so sure about it now. I think the first requirement for such a doubt to be seeded in one's mind is for the person to understand it first. What if they block all and any understanding of the issue before you even start? What if, in all likelihood, they don't understand your reasons and arguments to begin with? My experiences have shown me that the latter is usually the case. You are seen as the devil who is trying to lead the believer into sin and must be avoided at all cost. Whatever you are saying, by the same token, is nonsense and not worth even hearing. Their mind blocks out almost everything you say. They are totally consumed by the ways they are going to answer you, or the ways they are going to avoid you. This would be the full extend of the journey you can travel into a believer's religious mindset.

When they are set on answering you, they are not trying to address your concerns point by point. How can they, if they are not even hearing your points? What they are trying to do, instead, is to give you *an* answer, or better to say, *the* answer. Since they usually "know" the answer before you even ask your question, you have a very small chance to leave any positive impression on them, specially if you have poisoned the air with your sarcasm or any condescending remark whatsoever. You have lost the chance of having any rational conversation before you even started.

My argument against shock therapy is that because they do not hear you at all, you will not leave the effect you think you would, and you fling them into a dangerous orbit of regurgitation and reinforcing their false beliefs, now with vigour and determination. This is a lot more harmful to them and to the society as a whole, than to leave them alone and let them be exposed to the science and technology, impartially and disinterestedly, so they pick up the clues by themselves.

I will come back to this latter observation after the next title and will talk about self-initiated changes and the effects they can have on anyone.

Mystified

If I am to name the most challenging piece of intellectual human understanding that most humans have a hard time to comprehend, it has to be this:

> If we don't know the answer to a question, it does not mean that we can fill in the blanks with just any arbitrary story that we like.

It might sound funny or not too complex a concept, but most people who ever lived on this planet could never wrap their minds around it and will never do so. This seems to be the last stop for most people on earth. They just cannot get over this fact that if they don't know the answer then they cannot accept any just-so story as the answer.

Almost all members of *Homo sapiens* get stuck at this point and won't go any further.

How would they fill in the blank regardless of a question? The answer is usually a god! That's why it's called "the god of the gaps."

It is quite tragic that our species is unable of making this acknowledgement, i.e. to acknowledge that there are questions for which we don't have any answers yet, and the courage to leave it at that.

The incapacity to "leave it at that" is the grand cause of the most calamities brought upon us by ourselves. We seem not be able, in any meaningful way, to leave a blank, well, blank. If there is a black, then we feel an urge to fill it in with whatever comes to our mind. Our brains cannot properly function without assigning causes to the effects that it observes. It doesn't want to admit that: "I cannot figure that out at this point" and leave it to those who can, or try to find the answer without making up stories out of thin air.

"A universe without a god sounds ridiculous," someone might say. But think about it for a second. Which one is more ridiculous? Not knowing how all of these have started, or making up an obviously stupid, just-so story for no good reason and groundlessly claim that a hooligan, a monster, or a god made it all?

When things reach this point, the blood of most atheists start to boil. But wait a second. You expect a 100cm tall person to jump up ten-times their height, unaided? Who is more mistaken now?

I just told you that most people are not born with such a mental ability to accept unknowns as unknowns. They just cannot live with that. It's like this: most people are totally unable to see polarised light without special equipments. Or, humans cannot see ultraviolet light for as long as those eye-lenses are there (when it's removed, then they can, because the retina is sensitive to ultraviolet light but the lens absorbs it all). Many people are tone-deaf. Many others are colour-blind. Some people are tetrachromats, that is to say they have "four types of working cone cells, which means [they have] the ability to see far more colors than most of us can."[68] No human being is able to break down cellulose into sugar. They just can't. We don't have the right enzymes.

By the same token, if you expect most people to admit that they don't know how all of this started and leave it there, then you're less than informed.

Self-initiated change

We all want to change one another. The aim of this book has been to inform the readers of the many pitfalls that are ahead of attempts to change a wishful-thinker or a believer in myths and superstitions. We want to set them free from the chains of misinformation, deceptions, lies, violence, cruelties, and miseries that they impose upon human beings. This book has been about changing *things*, not others, for the better.

However, the reader has noticed that there are several problems at every turn in this journey. You have seen that any change is harder to make than to talk about. People have true, real, and strong reasons to cling to the only source of comfort their mothers taught them to seek. Although most people are smart enough to understand the force of evidence against their groundless religious beliefs, they have mountains of reasons not to do so actively and intentionally.

Our interventions usually backfire. Our interventions usually have the opposite effects. Our interventions usually do not have the effects we expect them to have. As you have seen in this book, reasons abound as for why believers won't listen and why what we get is usually a reverse effect.

Also, we have seen that solutions we can offer are not as effective as they should be. We don't have many tools to work with and this is a big problem.

Our tools are limited in number, in quality, and in depth. We do not possess, yet, any organization that publishes and freely distributes scientific alternative pamphlets at every corner in our cities. Religions do have them.

We do not have enough momentum to collect donations or to donate in the first place to run a big campaign that is effective, persistent, and regular. We haven't yet made countless places where secular individuals can regularly gather to have fun, to chat about their challenges, to seek professional help for free, to get emotional support, to party, to sing songs, to play organs, to dance, to get free courses on various topic, and to feel spiritual together. But believers do.

This is nothing that can be fixed overnight, but is something to put on the centre of every secular humanist's agenda now and going forth. These are systems, checks, and balances that we need to set in motion, and the time for them cannot come soon enough. Organization such as Recovering From Religion (at RecoveringFromReligion.org) must be supported, and technically and financially reinforced.

Nonetheless, there is one more issue that needs to be addressed: The change has to come from within (more on this later). As a Navajo proverb goes: "You can't wake a person who is pretending to be asleep" and as Voltaire would have said: "It is difficult to free fools from the chains they revere."

Most effective strategies are those that initiate a search within the individual, so they become the agent of changes to come. Unless they do it themselves, positive change would be very hard to bring about.

When people believe that *they* have come to a conclusion, in oppose to believing that *you* have forced them into a corner where they had no other choice but to admit a particular conclusion, then they accept it. If they are forced into agreeing with your conclusion, with themselves as a passive bystander, they would discard it later.

Every single strategy that we devise has to go with this principle in its core. If you write a book for believers, not like this book, you must think of them as rational, respectable, and sensitive people whom you are trying to enable to think better and to improve their intellectual life. Because most believers actually are smart, respectable, and sensitive people who, like all of us, would not go by just any proposition if they have not arrived at them by themselves. That is a sign of rationality. If you cannot understand a position, you better stay away from it, at least until you understand it for yourself.

Whether you are a teacher, a mother, a sister, a friend, a random guy on the street, a customer, or a "street epistemologist," you cannot afford to lose smart people to toxic conversations. The loss to the society would be huge. We cannot afford such losses.

We, atheists, are everywhere. We are in schools, in governments, in shopping malls, and in aeroplanes. We wear every hat you can imagine, we are engineers, dancers, lovers, mothers and fathers, friends and even enemies. Whatever we do has effects. If we scare a believer away from common sense and freethinking, we are responsible. If we poison conversations with sarcasm, condescension, mockery, and disrespectful attitudes, we are responsible. We are responsible to the society, to those who came before us and those who will come after us. We are responsible to ourselves and to everyone who lives on this planet. If we make rationality-averse individuals with our careless strategies, we are causing damage and leaving negative effects on others.

We cannot tolerate irrationality because we are secular humanists who respect truth, reality, and humanity above all. And, at the same time, we cannot afford to lose our friends and family members to religious beliefs. We have to cut our losses, and we have to do it fast, smart, and with utmost respect and tact. The future of our planet depends on us. It matters if we fail or succeed. We are all in it together.

PART TWO

What to do and what not to do

> "I contend we are both atheists, I just believe in one fewer god than you do. When you understand why you dismiss all other possible gods, you will understand why I dismiss yours."[69]
> — Stephen F Roberts

In this part of the book I am going to discuss a few challenges, principles, and misconceptions along with my advice to deal with them in real-world situations.

Selective Atheism

Let me define this term for the first time. "**Selective atheism**" is the lack of belief in the existence of at least one deity of your choice. So, a selective atheist is a person who does not believe that a given deity or deities exist. This includes almost all human beings, as long as there is at least one or more deities the existence of which they dismiss.

As nonbeliever as you

Help them understand that, in a sense, they are as atheists as you are.

How is that possible? There is no believer who believes in all and every supposed deity that has ever existed and will come to be in the future. Every single believer, is a total disbeliever of most other gods and goddesses that have littered the history. Every theist is an a-theists regarding almost all deities, a selective atheist. The god of their fathers or tribe is the only one that they worship.

If you are lucky enough, you might be able to make them see this fact. Also, if you are lucky, you can make them realize the fact that most other people on earth reject their version of gods and think that *their* stories are silly, baseless, and childish. Ironically enough, the oppositions do have valid arguments against a given deity. The task in hand is to make them see those arguments and to understand that there *are* strong objections against their particular deity.

The best you can do is to show them clearly that if everyone has sound arguments against everyone else's deity, then all deities are refuted.

My advice: break your discussion into smaller pieces in which you can demonstrate, case by case, that they, your audience, do not believe in other deities. Bring up the reasons why they refuse to believe in other deities.

Then show them how others see and judge their beloved religion Z. Show arguments advanced by the rival religions, *a*, *b*, *c*, etc. that clearly refute the claims in their religion Z.

Also, systematically demonstrate that their arguments against other religions, *a*, *b*, *c*, etc., also apply to their own religion, Z, as well. Explain the concept of **double-standard**, and make sure that they are on the same page as you are regarding the uniform application of arguments to the rivals' religions as well as their own religion Z.

If they demand evidence from other religions, hold their own claims against the same level of standard. If they are not convinced that certain events claimed by other religions can ever happen, then show them that the same applies to the claims that their own religion makes. If they use logical arguments against the existence of a particular deity, then show them that the same logical argument applies to their own deity as well.

This way, demonstrate to them that they are a selective atheist regarding other deities, therefore they perfectly know what it means to be an atheist.

They know all about you

> "We are all atheists, some of us just believe in fewer gods than others."[69]
> — Stephen F Roberts

Help them realize that they already know everything there is to know about atheism.

A theist says, "There is a god." An atheist says, "Prove it!"

That is all there is about being an atheist. An atheist does not believe in alternative supernatural systems of beliefs instead. He doesn't have any ritual, any deity, anything or anyone to worship, a particular book, or a school of thought. An atheist is simply a person who demands proofs for incredible claims. That is all there is to it.

My advice: Try to make it clear that atheism is not a system of thought, nor is it a particular set of beliefs. Atheism is a persistent search for evidence and proof for outlandish claims that theists make.

By virtue of this, all believers know exactly what it means to be an atheist, simply because they are atheists in all other occasions against other religions. There is no hidden wrinkle in this equation that believers can legitimately think they don't understand. They can understand the concept of atheism clearly and perfectly. The reason for that is that every single person on this planet is already a selective atheist, is born an atheist, and is practising atheism every single day with no exception. Everyone who has ever lived is, at least, a selective atheist and knows *all* there is about it inside-out.

Don't let your audience read anything else into an atheistic position; because, there is none. It is very common, almost like a second nature, amongst believers to attribute a set of beliefs to atheists as if atheists have a guideline, a holy book, or a manual, according to which they operate.

When a believer says Stalin killed millions of innocent people, and he was an atheist, they are shamelessly suggesting that Stalin did so *because* he was following some sort of instruction, namely atheism, and killed people based on them; which is obviously nonsensical. No one can justify killing innocent people based on the need for proof for extraordinary claims. No one has ever gone around and said, "You said there is a god? Prove it!" and then start killing others based on that. This argument against atheism is as foolish as arguments can get.

Stalin was an atheist. That means, amongst other things, he needed extraordinary proofs before being able to believe in extraordinary claims. That is all there is about Stalin's atheism.

Stalin, also, was a brutal criminal like many other criminals in history. His criminality was not based on 'Show me proofs for theism or else I will kill you.' His criminality was based on ill ideologies and a sick mind.

In comparison, when we look at what ISIS or ISIL has done to the people of Syria and Iraq, you can clearly see that what they have done is done exactly and only *because* of their religious convictions.[70] It was their faith, their religious convictions, that gave them a licence to kill thousands of Yazidis (see the article called Genocide of Yazidis by ISIL on Wikipedia).[71]

Atheists don't have a book to refer to, no text to interpret, no creed to issue, no set of ideologies to follow. Religions, most of them, do have all of these items and more.

An insane, atheist dictator does not go around and kill others because they believe in gods or because they are religious. Even if he or she did so, it is not different from going around and killing everyone who does not like vanilla milkshakes. There is nothing in atheism that orders anyone to kill, or even suggests anything to that effect. "Prove your claim!" is not an excuse for any action whatsoever. If a person decides to commit a crime *based* on the principles of atheism, they are patently insane for the simple fact that atheism does not have a set of principles.

Atheism, in general, is a reaction towards theists' extraordinary claims. As 'lack of theism', atheism does not claim anything, does not deny anything, does not claim knowledge of anything, and does not imply the existence or non-existence of anything (based on sound arguments, positive atheists do;[72,73] a topic that is beyond the scope of this book[74]). The position of an atheist can be summarised in the position of a person who would say the following upon hearing an incredible claim. "Oh yeah? That is incredible!

Do you have any scientific evidence for what you are saying? I am all ears."

"Let's kill all believers," might actually be uttered by an insane nonbeliever. But, how would that be the result of a stance against extraordinary claims? How would that count as a result of atheism? People with and without a fear of the afterlife committed unspeakable crimes. It has never been the interpretation of atheism that made them do so. Stalin never argued that since there is no afterlife in which he would be punished, he was going to kill millions of innocent people. If the fear of an afterlife could keep people from committing crimes, ISIL members would have never committed any crime, but they have.[71]

> "With or without religion, good people can behave well and bad people can do evil; but for good people to do evil — that takes religion."[75]
> — Steven Weinberg

Don't let believers push you into holes that have nothing to do with your actual position. Insist on the actual meaning of "atheism" and stay on message. Don't let them pretend they don't know about atheism, or they need to learn about it before they can say anything. They know perfectly well all there is about atheism. Basically, because there is nothing to know about it, and because, they are one, themselves.

Emotions

You cannot argue with emotions. You cannot convince 'emotions' of anything.

If it happened that the true anchor of someone's beliefs is in emotions, then it is only wise not to pick up an already lost battle with them. Emotions do not come by the means of careful reflections, investigative, or scientific research. Because of that, they will not go away by those means either.

Emotions are trivially easy to evoke and gravely hard to forget. Once they are there, they are there to stay. If the source of one's holding on to a belief is tightly woven in a net of emotions, if they are created or held due to strong emotions, then there would be virtually impenetrable to any alteration by arguments or evidence. Wisdom demotes when emotions emote.

My advice: Leave them in peace. Wish them well and let them be.

Your intervention: It can backfire and potentially cause more harm than good. Not only will you not change their mind, but also you run the risk of making them irritated and more stubborn in their delusions. You can also hurt their feelings.

If you attack a feeling, even unknowingly, you hurt the person. They will genuinely be hurt and it would make them distance even further away from such things as whatever you are offering, lest they might be hurt again.

"Playing Chess with a Pigeon"

> "Debating creationists on the topic of evolution is rather like trying to play chess with a pigeon; it knocks the pieces over, craps on the board, and flies back to its flock to claim victory."[76]
> — Scott D. Weitzenhoffer

Are you feeling that you are gradually losing your ground? It's because you have already lost it.

This doesn't mean that theists' arguments are sound and strong. Not at all. I have yet to see one that can stand a fair trial. The reason why you are feeling that you are losing an argument is because the way you have approached and handled it has not been suitable for that situation from the start.

The moment a theist starts to use a moving-the-goalposts[77–79] arguing style, you have already lost *any* and *all* arguments that follow. Unless you fully stop the dialogue and make sure that everyone knows very clearly what the theist is doing, there is no point in taking another step forward at all. No step in any direction would take you anywhere anyway.

Watch any of the "discussions" that prominent atheists have had over the past years with theists on YouTube. There are hundreds of them. Most of them, if not all, are completely futile. The reason is that the theist claims Y, the atheist tries to address or refute Y. The theist moves on to claiming Z before the previous discussion of Y reaches any conclusion. Then the atheist moves on to address Z with sound arguments. Before anything is even properly discussed and start to make any sense, the theist jumps to X, W, G, and N. The atheist tries to address G and N. The theist jumps to M and H and then on and on. The results? Humiliated and disoriented, dashing in the dark to defeat a devil the size of a dime that disappears at will.

My advice: Stop the conversation the moment the goalpost is moved. Call the fallacy of *Moving the Goalposts* and stay there. Refuse to move any further unless the practice of moving the goalposts is stopped. There won't be *any* point in keeping a never-concluding dialogue going on anyway. There is no way to win any argument that its proponent would not accept any conceivable evidence as its refutation. So, don't bother with the rest of the game the theist wants to squeeze you into.

Bring everything back over and over to the first point of contention and demand clear and conclusive answer to your rebuttal of the first point. Demand surrender for the first battle fought before moving to the next.

Notice that it is not enough to make a great rebuttal and stick to it. You have already made the rebuttal and it is already been ignored. The problem is not the rebuttal nor is it the evidence you are presenting. The problem that you are distracted to overlook is that you are being ignored. Therefore, bring the whole game to a halt and make sure this very nasty game of moving the goalposts is stopped. Unless it is properly dealt with, there is no point discussing *anything* else.

Define the defeating conditions

More importantly, as soon as you caught a fallacy, make sure that you and your audience agree, one hundred percent, upon what exactly would constitute a counter argument or a counter example against their position that can, in principle, refute their claim. Under what circumstance would they agree that their argument was false? Unless this condition is clearly uttered and accepted by both sides, any further step would be totally futile. Ask them, 'What would count as the rebuttal of their claim?' And don't let that go until they acknowledged that you have successfully met their criteria (of course if it is achievable to begin with).

Here is another way to think about it. Ask them 'What should I show you, what evidence should I bring up, what kind of proof do you need, so when I deliver it to you, then you will agree that you were wrong in this particular claim?'

If their answer is 'Nothing can change my mind,' then you two are not discussing anything. They are asserting their claims and you are asserting yours. There is no dialogue here.

On the other hand, if they say, 'Show me this and that, and my claim will be defeated,' then, if they are asking for something deliverable, not something impossible to deliver, then hold them accountable for this agreement. Once you delivered, then call them on the previous agreement and stop. Don't go one step further. Stay there until they get on the same page as you are. Otherwise, you are wasting everyone's time and energy.

Define the terms

This is closely related to the issue of moving the goalposts. One reason why theists can easily change their criteria on how and when their claims are effectively refuted is vagueness and obscurity of the terms their claims rely on. They either do it out of malice or ignorance.

You ask them, 'Show me the evidence!' And they show you what they think would count as their "evidence." Then you clearly demonstrate that their "evidence" does not prove what they attempted to prove and show them why. Then instead of admitting defeat, they massage their "evidence" into a different concept and then claim that, 'Tad-da! It works now!' You demonstrate that it is still falling short of being a viable proof. And they change it again. This game can go forever.

Let's have a look at the Noah's Arc example. There is no possible way that any such thing can be remotely possible to be built either with the Noah's technology or our today's technology. There is no way any future generation would be able to achieve such a goal either. It is trivial to know why. Just count the number of known insects and other animals. Multiply that number by 2. Then try to figure out how much space each pair would take for accommodation. You will quickly learn that there is no way any construction can possibly collect them all. It is only a grade 5 mathematics calculation. Then add the time to get them together (not all of them can be found on one continent, let alone one country). The time and space to do anything like what is suggested in the story is prohibitively enormous. Also, the structure to accommodate such a collection of living organisms certainly cannot be a plain floating ship.

How, then, can anyone honestly believe that the Noah's story is a true story? Your theist friend, of course, would easily beg to differ. They would reply, probably, by saying that the ship was "big" and the animals were called to come over to the ship by god, so Noah didn't have to gather them in one place.

Anything is possible in a mythical story. Time and space are not limited. Events can happen incredibly faster than they actually happen in the real world. Impossible things happen with ease and regularity. Borders, limits, logic, and consistency do not play any role. Living beings can live for much longer than they actually can live in reality. The list goes on and on. Rules don't apply to mythical elements of mythical stories. This is why anything can happen in these stories.

To bring the believer down to reality from the clouds they are dwelling in, you might ask them what they meant by "big" and "god." Since their story is a myth, their "big" also turns out to be a myth. No matter how conclusively you demonstrate to them that a working ship would not be "big" enough to accommodate all of the animals, they will still claim a "bigger" ship. When you are not limited by any law of the nature, there wouldn't be any limit to your "big."

Unless terms such as "big" and "god" in a story like that is clearly defined and the people involved in the conversation adhere to their definitions, there won't be any end to such conversations. No clear definition of terms used in claims can easily allow infinite room for theists' goalposts to move into.

When you mention the challenge of actually making such a "big" ship single-handedly, they would move backward and claim that it was not *that* big for Noah not to be able to build it. Here, the vague term is also "to build." Since in a conversation, "to build" is only a word and does not entail anything, they can use it anyway they like with no consequence. However, "to build" entails a lot of things. From a project management perspective, you will need to answer quite a few questions about the tools, resources, time, and energy needed to finish a monumental task like building a giant ship to accommodate a pair of all the animals on the planet. Ask any project manager, and they will quickly show you, on Gantt charts and tables, that such a task cannot possibly be completed by one person, nor can it be done by a family. The resources needed to complete such a task is simple beyond anything that even a town-full of people can muster in one generation. And yet, the theist believes that Noah did it on his own.

When you confront them with the problems that the term "to build" would impose to the story, they will change the size of the ship to something that *would* fit the possible resources then. Now, the "big" definition is back to save them. Now the ship is small enough for the man to "build" in a short period of time. So, whenever they have a problem with one aspect of the story, they move the sliders and knobs of other terms up and down so the final result becomes a fit. How convenient!

My advice: Since it is almost impossible to define all consequential terms in a claim in one setting, it would be almost impossible to avoid this problem you are going to have discussing anything with theists. Try to keep it short, simple, and documented.

As you go forward in a conversation, the number of magical words that would need defining increases dramatically. You will not be able to effectively keep track of all of them, not even the majority of them. If you allow the conversation to go wild, then you have invited yourself into a forest of vague, liquid, and wobbly terms and concepts that change instantly as per necessity. You won't be able to remember them all, let alone to address them all. This is exactly where the theists build their nests. You cannot touch the nest because the nest flies away any time you get close enough.

Write down as many terms and concepts as you can catch in the course of the conversation. Keep the concepts as short as possible. Try to deal with each individual issue before letting the flow of the conversation carry you out of your zone. Hold the theist to clear definitions. Write them down and keep them in front of both of you. Try to be specific with numbers, sizes, times, places, and anything that can be traced to reality (you won't be able to do anything with the items that have no root in reality).

Theists usually hate specificity, clear definitions, numbers, laws of nature, and anything rooted in reality. If you keep it real, you would probably ruin their fun, and they would likely abandon the conversation with the same enthusiasm that they started it. Be prepared for an abrupt stop in the conversation because if you try to be too clear, if you disperse too much of the clouds, the naked emperor would become too visible to everyone, and they don't like it. Be ready for them to quit at any time if you insist on the clarity of mind and demystified definitions.

Everyone is a selective atheist

And necessarily so. I discussed this before. Help them understand why they are every bit as much atheist as you are.

You are an atheist for exactly the same reasons that they are, although they cannot see it and don't admit it. You don't believe in "gods of new and old" for exactly the same reasons that they don't believe in a million or so gods out there in history. The only differences are that you know it, and that you don't see any evidence to exempt *their* particular brand of god or gods from the rest.

My advice: Try to draw their attention to the similarities between your view and theirs. Merely mentioning these similarities is not enough. 'Try to make them *see* that both of you are almost identical in the way you look at millions of gods.

You need to make them realize that they are using a double-standard when they turn to their own god. They can, with the help of your examples and careful demonstrations, see that they use the same logic and methodologies to discount million other gods that you do. You use the standards uniformly everywhere, whereas they pick and choose and have granted their god immunity. They cannot see the irony. If you are lucky, you might be able to help them see it for what it is.

Ask them what makes *their* god(s) so special and immune to the same standard of scrutiny. Show them why their favouritism cannot hold up by *their own* standards applied to other gods.

This task, nonetheless, would be way more challenging than you can even imagine. Next, I am going to tell you why.

You explained it; so what?

You can explain things to someone, but you cannot understand the explanations for them. Your 'explaining' does not automatically translate into their 'understanding.'

Try as hard as you may, due to many hard limits to humans' cognitive power, your efforts would not change those limits at all.

How hard is it to make a four-years old understand and appreciate the theory of General Relativity and the Quantum Field Theory? I am not sure if that would be possible at all (just to learn the mathematics needed to construct and understand those theories, one needs to spend more than four years learning math and physics). There might be a handful of genius toddlers here and there around the globe, but human babies, in general, are not capable of understanding such concepts.

The exact same is true with human adults. Babies' mental capacities grow as they grow older. However, it does not grow infinitely. Humans' mental capacity to understand things reaches a peak and then, after staying more or less in a plateau, it gradually declines after a certain age. That peak is not infinite. Such maximum performance falls comfortably under a normal, bell-curve distribution. Most people end up being somewhere in the middle of the bell curve. Some grow up to become geniuses and some simple-minded. Even the geniuses don't have infinite mental capacities. They also have a maximum performance in their abilities that is limited.

Humans, with these limited mental capacities, might try to understand different concepts. Average people would succeed at grasping concepts with average complexity or difficulty (after all, "average" difficulty is defined just as a difficulty level at which average people would be able to grasp it if they try hard enough).

The grave mistake we all might make when we try to explain a concept to others is to assume that the audience is *average* in all of their mental capacities, and they *would* understand such a concept if we try hard enough. Sometimes the assumption is even worse: that the audience is above the average while the topic at hand is assumed to have an average or below average difficulty.

We all do that. Once we grasp a concept, we automatically start to see its difficulty level as average or even easy, depending on how much effort we had to put into understanding it. Then when it comes time to explain it to someone else, we automatically make two assumptions: 1- The topic is not that hard to grasp and, 2- Our audience is smart enough to grasp it. Neither of these two assumptions might necessarily be true in a given case.

My advice: Don't assume that your audience would understand your points should you put enough resources into explaining those points to them. It might never happen.

Such mistaken assumptions are the constant source of frustration and energy waste. If you cannot make a five-years old child understand your topic, the chances are that some of your believer audiences would eventually fall short of understanding your points altogether.

Before you start explaining anything to your audience, ask yourself the following questions:

- is my point easy enough for a five-year-old to get? If yes, then

- can I explain it to a five-year-old well enough for them to get it? If yes, then

- is my audience's mental capacity as good or better than a five-year-old child?

If the answer to any of these questions is a "No," then I suggest dropping the endeavour altogether.

The problem with those questions is that you might not be able to correctly estimate the answer to the third question. Although, mental capacities have strong, positive correlations with age, nevertheless, knowing one's age does not necessarily tell you the level of their mental capacities. The older a person is, the more likely they are to have reached the peak performance of the mental capacity of an average adult. But, they might not be average to begin with, and their age alone does not tell you that.

Unfortunately, the life achievements of a person does not do it either. One can be a feeble-minded clown and still end up being a politician (the 45th president of the USA comes to mind). Being a politician, therefore, might have very little to do with their mental capabilities, and a lot to do with the propaganda, heritage and inheritance, fashion, or look that made them rich and famous. The fact that a person can make a lot of money, or hold a high office, or be popular and famous, is not necessarily a function of their intelligence and does not tell enough about their mental abilities.

Therefore, you are on your own to guestimate the wit of your audience in a few seconds or minutes before engaging in a costly conversation that may or may not help them understand your point.

Incentives

When money is at stake, no rebuttal is good enough.

This one is an easy case to deal with. If you are dealing with a person who is motivated by any kind of monetary incentives, you are totally out of luck. There would be nothing that you might say, demonstrate, or produce that would change their mind. Even if they change their mind in private, there is no way that they would admit it in public. Admitting their logical mistakes and their lack of evidence to support their delusion equals the crumbling of their monetary gains. In many cases such losses can be huge and totally devastating to the defender of baseless, religious convictions.

People are not isolated objects. They have ties, motivations, connections, plans, needs, and ways of fulfilling those needs. The ties they might have with other people might be their only source of income. Their connections with others might be the bread and butter of their lives. Their short-term and long-term plans might totally rely on the predictable outcomes of their connections and ties to others. Their basic needs might not be met at all if those ties are severed and connections damaged. Such is the case for many believers. It's not just them. It's a whole universe around them that makes them adhere to a belief system, however absurd that belief might sound.

These and many more are the reasons why organizations such as Recovering from Religion are created.

> "Recovering from Religion (RR) is an international non-profit organisation, that helps people who have left or are in the process of leaving religion to deal with any impacts of leaving their faith by creating support groups, providing a telephone hotline for "people in their most urgent time of need," as well as offering a range of online tools and practical resources."[80]

The way to approach the cases where a "believer" is actually taken hostage by their network of interrelated economic, social, and emotional circumstances is totally different from most other cases. For example, a priest or preacher who does not believe in religion any more but cannot leave it just yet due to the huge, negative, and painful consequences of their leave, cannot drop the facade of their stance as easily as one can drop a belief in a mistaken mathematical equation.

In the former case, leaving the facade means a lot of trouble. It changes their lives immediately and will destabilize their livelihood, their family, their job, their current social status, and their future. They might lose their lives as they know it altogether.

In the latter case, it is expected of the person who believes in an erroneous mathematical equation to drop it as soon as they learn about the error. If others find out that a mathematician still adheres to an incorrect mathematical proof for instance, the mathematician's reputation would be tarnished and the consequences of not letting go of the falsehood can cost the mathematician their job or social status. This is virtually the opposite of the former case.

In the former case, one might lose everything if they let go of a falsehood. In the latter case one might lose a lot if they don't let go of a falsehood. You cannot approach these two cases using the same strategy.

And still there are many more cases of "believers" where they don't actually believe in anything they preach, but they are not planning to demolish the delusion, because it is the delusion that brings them fame, power, sex, money, and everything else. They love the deception and fight you to their teeth to stop you from destroying their business.

If you come across the deceiver kind, which in my opinion is the most harmful kind of human beings, then you would have absolutely zero chance of changing anything with them by debating or arguing with them. William L. Craig is an example of such fraud who has built a carrier out of his deceptions. He doesn't lie through his teeth because he genuinely believes in those lies. He also doesn't do it merely because he is stuck in a corner where he doesn't believe in the absurdities he spreads around, but cannot get out either. He commits the fraud that he has been working on for years specially because it is bringing him fame, power, prestige, money, and other things that you and I might not ever know about. He loves what he is doing. He also knows that he is bullshitting,81 and yet he does it anyway with joy, rigour, and determination.

> "A **charlatan** (also called **swindler** or **mountebank**) is a person practising quackery or some similar confidence trick in order to obtain money, fame or other advantages via some form of pretense or deception."[82]

William is the best example of a contemporary charlatan, a professional bullshitter.[83–85]

My advice: First determine which type of "believer" you are dealing with in terms of socio-economic incentives.

If you are dealing with a true believer, which would be more likely, then you might proceed by having a dialogue with them and there might be a slight chance of actually getting somewhere.

If your "believer" is actually a socio-economic hostage of their situation, then your approach must be different. You probably don't need a lot of persuading, refutation, evidence, and arguments. They already know them to some extent. What they need, instead, is lots and lots of support of all kinds. Refer them to an organization such as Recovering from Religion. They are equipped with many social supports and tools for people trapped in this category to make a much less damaging transition.

If you are dealing with a W. Craig type of charlatan, then run; as fast as you can. Don't waste a second of your time to discuss anything with a Craig. Craigs are, by definition, running a business out of what they preach. They are not going to demolish their business just because you asked them to. Run![86]

Flooding a debate

> "The **Gish Gallop** (also known as **proof by verbosity**) is the fallacious debate tactic of drowning your opponent in a flood of individually-weak arguments in order to prevent rebuttal of the whole argument collection without great effort. The Gish Gallop is a belt-fed version of the on the spot fallacy,[87] as it's unreasonable for anyone to have a well-composed answer *immediately* available to every argument present in the Gallop. The Gish Gallop is named after creationist Duane Gish, who often abused it."[81]

Flooding a debate with shotgun debris of scattered quasi-arguments, in conjunction with moving the goalposts makes any conversation with some religion apologists worse than chasing the wind. Since it is only a game they are interested in playing, and not actually exchanging ideas and learning anything, you can never have any constructive discussion with them; at all.

If you remember from Eric Bern's book called *Games People Play*,[88] there is a common game called "Yes, but." It has no end and is not played to be useful, helpful, constructive, or otherwise fruitful in any way. It is played by at least two players. One suggests possible solutions and the other player, no matter what the solution was, always says, "Yes, but..." and they continue to tell the first player why the solution is of no use and why the problem stays unsolved. The player with the problem-solving role might try as hard as they can. No solution is going to be accepted even if one or more of them were excellent solutions to the problem. Hence, the game goes round and round ad infinitum. At the end of the game, which is when everyone is too exhausted to keep playing it and the solution-generating player simply gives up, the solution-denying player would come out triumphant, rejecting and deflecting all and every attempt to solve their problem. Now they can proudly feel vindicated in their feeling miserable or helpless. Now they feel they are the legitimate owner of an unsolvable problem, and they can use this negative charge later as a currency to justify doing a bad thing. Most apologists' game-playing strategies are squarely based on the "Yes, but..." game, even if they don't utter this exact phrase.

When a debate is flooded by bogus arguments, baseless claims, and rapid firing of nonsenses, no matter how smart and fast you are, you won't be able to keep up with the flood. There is a reason why it is called a flood.

> **Bullshit asymmetry principle:**
> "The amount of energy needed to refute bullshit is an order of magnitude bigger than to produce it."
> — Alberto Brandolini

You might try to address one, two, or three of the baseless claims, but since they keep coming, you will finally be overwhelmed. You will fall behind and the observing audience would, unconsciously, take it as your inability to address the raised points. What they will not realize is how ridiculous the whole game is and how baseless the claims are. But none of these matter to the unsuspecting audience. What they actually see is that you are gradually falling behind, and then almost totally washed away by the deluge of claims. The fact that none of the claims have any merit would not attract their attention as much as the fact that you are not able to address them effectively any more does. In the end, the apologist claims victory, whether or not they actually won anything, and you will be seen as, well, the loser of the two. If the one side said they won, then what would be the status of the other side in a zero-sum game?

My advice: Under no circumstance should you engage in any debate of any kind with a person who is known as one who floods debates with their baseless claims. They will not allow any manageable number of claims to be addressed step by step and the whole point of the game they are playing is to claim victory at the end regardless of the debate.

Debate flooding is a very disrespectful way of "debating" anything with an opponent. No one should stoop so low to the level of such charlatans who use this game in all of their "debates." It is an insult to others who are participating in the debate and the ones who are watching it. What these apologists do is an insult to human intellect and to anyone interested in truth.[83-85] Avoid them at all cost.

If you want to see an actual footage of a debate between a religion apologist and a philosopher, a thinker, a scientist, or any number of reputable person, then search the Internet. There are literally hundreds, if not thousands, of such "debates" on YouTube.

Let's take the case of William's alleged "debates" with actual thinkers. If you search the following keywords on YouTube:

Christopher Hitchens and William Craig

You will even find full-length footages of such presentations. By watching any of those footages, you will clearly see how William responds to any rebuttal by Hitchens. He actually doesn't! Instead of addressing Hitchens' concerns or refutations, he brings up yet another claim, almost totally irrelevant to what was discussed, and then another one, and another one until his time is up. In turn, Hitchens, whom by this time has addressed a few of the first baseless claims, is beginning to get disoriented. He tries to focus on one of the tens of bogus claims by William till his time is up. William's turn repeats exactly the previous cycle again. He starts another, totally unrelated deluge of nonsense until his time is over. When these waves of utter nonsense hit Hitchens, or any other thinker or philosopher for that matter, they finally become totally disoriented, go on tangent, and, in their own minds, think that they are participating in the same show as William's. The truth is that they are not.

Witnessing such a scene is disturbing. It occurs almost always between William and any other poor soul who has happened to be lured to have a "debate" with the trickster. Some smart thinkers actually refused to even appear on the same stage as such a conman.[86] But this is an exception rather than a rule. Even very smart people, such as Sam Harris, have fallen into that trap.[89]

At any rate, if you need to see for yourself examples of what I am talking about, do a YouTube search as I described above and also see the bibliography section and the end of this book. The power of the evidence before your eyes would be much more than anything I can come up with in words.

Changed their mind? Nope!

We don't change anyone's mind. They do it themselves.

Let's say you have made your audience truly understand your points. You made them arrive at the same conclusion that followed logically from your principles. What if they don't want to change their mind?

We automatically assume that as soon as a person understands a principle and its implications, they would immediately change their mind on how they were dealing with the real-world consequences of their newly discovered knowledge, jump the ship, and start implementing the principles and their implications in their lives. We assume that they then throw their mistaken beliefs out of the window. In reality, however, none of these usually happen.

I have witnessed the transformation of two deeply religious, close friends. They changed from their old and baseless beliefs to rational and non-theistic world-views over two conversations that I had with someone *else* at their presence. I was not even talking to those two friends, let alone attempting to change their minds. I didn't want to, and didn't care to, change *their* minds. I was talking to someone else, for Zeus' sake, while my friends were passively listening, each in separate occasions. I don't even know how *they* flipped whereas those whom I was talking to and wanted to flip or at least wanted to understand my points never did. The bystanders changed whereas my target group kept their delusions even more firmly after our conversation was over.

The switch from being deeply religious to being atheists happened in both occasions so suddenly, so out of the blue, and over such a short period of time, and, in my mind, over such trivial topics that for a long time I was totally sceptical of their real transformation. In both cases I couldn't believe my eyes, their reactions, and the fact that, in all improbabilities, it was my input into a conversation with someone else that really changed my friends. My inner voice was shouting: "You've gotta be kidding me!"

To this day, I never learned what I said that caused them to rethink their beloved convictions and change their minds. If anything, I would have told you that,

"Probably there was nothing I could have told them that could change their mind."

But, there I was, astonished at what I was witnessing, looking at friends who were transforming before my eyes. It was literally like watching a very elaborate domino set-up start to change from a humble topple of one tiny piece and snowball into an enormous transformation. The fall of one piece made the fall of thousand pieces possible.

I never saw that coming. I never learned whence cometh the first fall, the first flip. Which piece started it all? Nonetheless, I could see it going through the domino forest of my friends' thoughts and beliefs and flipping the pieces rapidly and unexpectedly. I was asking myself: "Did *I* do that? How did *that* happen?"

I wish I knew how those sparks in a gunpowder storage started. How those explosive transformations started in the minds of those two friends of mine. Although I might never learn how that happened, I learned one thing for sure. That I didn't actively change their minds. They did. Many other people heard exactly the same words, the same conversations that my two friends did. Those people never changed much (not that I know of). The mystery is that some didn't get most of my points, but some did. And the lesson was that it was mostly their own work.

Someone much smarter and more hard-working than me might figure it all out one day. However, I am not holding my breath for it to happen anytime soon.

My advice: Don't bother entertaining the nagging thought of who would get it and who wouldn't. That is not what you can control. You almost have zero control over such outcomes. It's not a classroom, you are not a teacher, your audiences are not your students, and they are not going to be evaluated at the end of the semester to see who got it and who didn't. Your pay-check would not be adjusted according to the results. You will not be held responsible for those who didn't get your points and those who did. Simply try to be genuine, authentic, authoritative, principled, and brief to the point.

More often than not you won't even notice who is really paying attention to the substance of your arguments instead of merely waiting for their turn to answer you and defeat you as good as they can.

Be ready to support your claims with evidence or else don't make them altogether. Try to play the role of an articulate, informative, kind, and respectful interviewer, journalist, broadcaster, or moderator. All you are doing, whether you like it or not, is broadcasting your case based on logic, scientific methods, and evidence that are rooted in reality. The moment you start to think of yourself as a teacher or an illuminator, you start losing your audience. Plus you are wasting your mental energy into a useless pit that only makes you more enemies by means of putting others on defensive.

Don't forget that only what *can* happen would happen. Those whose minds are ready to change would get the points and would change. Those whose time has not come yet, would not change. And there is almost nothing you can do to change it.

> "Woe to him who teaches men faster than they can learn."[90]
> — Will Durant

All we can do

These are all we can hope to achieve in a conversation with a believer. No conversion, de-conversion, and no persuasion is possible.

People do not intend to participate in most conversations to be persuaded about how wrong or misguided they have been. They are not there to be told that you know things that they don't, nor that they need to re-evaluate their fundamental beliefs.

You might be able to convince someone that a gas-station is not where they thought it was, and if you are right, then you can show them where it actually is on a map and in the real world on a street. Then, it is possible to double-check your assertions, to ask others to test them and see if you were right, and to investigate the matter through an impartial investigator. A reality-check can be done easily and conclusively and the matter can be settled beyond any doubt. However, the situation is not the same with metaphysical and religious claims, beliefs, and assertions.

With religious beliefs, you are up against a much more subjective and intangible challenge. Given you are absolutely correct, it is more like trying to convince an adult that a certain cherished, childhood memory of theirs, of which they are proud, is false; that the events in the "memory" had never actually happened in reality; that they had always been wrong all along. Good luck with that.

In a glance

Here are the traps you want to **avoid**:
- *ad hominem* attack[23]
- verbal harassment (e.g. mean comments)
- offensive and insulting words
- condescending tone
- unsolicited comments or advice
- sarcasm, ridicule
- chasing a moving goalpost
- salvaging a flooded debate

Here are a few things you want to **stick to** at all time:
- facts
- evidence
- demand for evidence
- respect, and demand for respect
- courtesy
- benefit of doubt
- 5-years old audience assumption
- asking questions
- listening more than you speak
- determining a falsification threshold
- demanding clear definitions
- lowering your expectations

Bibliography

1 Anon (n.d.) 'A quote by Jorge Luis Borges'. *Goodreads.* [online] Available from: https://goo.gl/zMPHzV (Accessed 29 March 2018)

2 Stone, Jon R. (2006) *The Routledge Book of World Proverbs*, Routledge.

3 Loftus, Elizabeth (2013) *How reliable is your memory?*, TEDGlobal. [online] Available from: https://www.ted.com/talks/elizabeth_loftus_the_fiction_of_memory (Accessed 29 March 2018)

4 Winter, Alison (2012) *Memory: fragments of a modern history*, Chicago, University of Chicago Press.

5 McDermott, Kathleen B. and Chan, Jason C. K. (2004) 'False Memories', in Byrne, J. H. (ed.), *Learning and Memory*, New York, Macmillan Reference USA, pp. 145–147. [online] Available from: https://goo.gl/TUh86e (Accessed 29 March 2018)

6 Newberg, Andrew B, D'Aquili and Rause (2002) *Why God won't go away: brain science and the biology of belief*, New York, Ballantine.

7 Akkad, Omar El. (2009) 'This is your brain on religion'. *The Globe and Mail.* [online]

Available from: https://www.theglobeandmail.com/technology/science/this-is-your-brain-on-religion/article1154556/ (Accessed 30 March 2018)

8   Boyer, Pascal (2002) *Religion Explained* Reprint., Basic Books.

9   Bright, Eric (2009) *Religovirology: Meme Mechanics, Virology of Religion, and Refutation of Supernaturalism*, New York, iUniverse.

10 Russell, Bertrand (2010) *Why I am not a Christian: and other essays on religion and related subjects*, London [u.a., Routledge.

11 Hume, David (1998) *Dialogues Concerning Natural Religion* 2 edition. Popkin, R. H. (ed.), Indianapolis, Hackett Publishing Company, Inc.

12 Nyhan, Brendan and Reifler, Jason (2010) 'When Corrections Fail: The Persistence of Political Misperceptions'. *Political Behavior*, 32(2), pp. 303–330.

13 Chen, Frances S., Minson, Julia A., Schöne, Maren and Heinrichs, Markus (2013) 'In the Eye of the Beholder Eye Contact Increases Resistance to Persuasion'. *Psychological Science*, p. 0956797613491968.

14 Plait, Phil (2010) *Phil Plait - Don't Be A Dick*, Las Vegas, The Amaz!ng Meeting 8. [online]

Available from: https://vimeo.com/13704095 (Accessed 29 March 2018)

15 Plait, Phil (2010) 'Don't Be a Dick, Part 1: the video: Bad Astronomy'. *DISCOVERmagazine.com.* [online] Available from: http://blogs.discovermagazine.com/badastronomy/2010/08/17/dont-be-a-dick-part-1-the-video/ (Accessed 29 March 2018)

16 Plait, Phil (2010) 'Don't Be a Dick, Part 2: links: Bad Astronomy'. *DISCOVERmagazine.com.* [online] Available from: http://blogs.discovermagazine.com/badastronomy/2010/08/18/dont-be-a-dick-part-2-links/ (Accessed 29 March 2018)

17 Bryant, Jennings, Brown, Dan and Parks, Sheri L. (1981) 'Ridicule as an educational corrective.' *Journal of Educational Psychology,* 73(5), pp. 722–727.

18 Zuwerink Jacks, Julia and Cameron, Kimberly A. (2003) 'Strategies for Resisting Persuasion'. *Basic and Applied Social Psychology,* 25(2), pp. 145–161.

19 Friesen, Justin P., Campbell, Troy H. and Kay, Aaron C. (2014) 'The Psychological Advantage of Unfalsifiability: The Appeal of Untestable Religious and Political Ideologies'. *Journal of*

Personality and Social Psychology, p. No Pagination Specified.

20 O'Grady, Cathleen (2014) 'Why do we cling to beliefs when they're threatened by facts?' *Ars Technica*. [online] Available from: https://goo.gl/g8Yiyl (Accessed 29 March 2018)

21 Anon (2011) *Why Are You Atheists So Angry? Greta Christina Skepticon 4*, [online] Available from: https://youtu.be/GUI_ML1qkQE (Accessed 29 March 2018)

22 Nietzsche, Friedrich (1989) *Beyond Good & Evil: Prelude to a Philosophy of the Future*, New York, Vintage.

23 Graham, Paul (2008) 'How to Disagree'. [online] Available from: https://goo.gl/wqwGWB (Accessed 25 March 2018)

24 Ehrman, Bart D (2011) *Forged: writing in the name of God: why the Bible's authors are not who we think they are*, New York, HarperOne.

25 Leurent, B., Nazareth, I., Bellón-Saameño, J., Geerlings, M.-I., et al. (2013) 'Spiritual and religious beliefs as risk factors for the onset of major depression: an international cohort study'. *Psychological Medicine*, FirstView, pp. 1–12.

26 Anon (n.d.) 'Opportunity Cost'. *Oxford dictionary (American English)*. [online] Available from: https://en.oxforddictionaries.com/definition/us/opportunity_cost (Accessed 29 March 2018)

27 Anon (n.d.) 'Opportunity Cost'. *Inc.com*. [online] Available from: https://www.inc.com/encyclopedia/opportunity-cost.html (Accessed 29 March 2018)

28 Anon (2008) 'Opportunity Cost'. *Encyclopedia of Management*, pp. 645–646.

29 Anon (2013) *Jerry DeWitt - Interview with We Are Atheism*, [online] Available from: https://youtu.be/zpmvIxfqYmY (Accessed 29 March 2018)

30 Friedrich, Sandra L. (2003) 'Denial', in Harris, M. and Thackerey, E. (eds.), *The Gale Encyclopedia of Mental Disorders*, Detroit, Gale, pp. 281–283. [online] Available from: https://goo.gl/q2uIma (Accessed 29 March 2018)

31 Darity, William A., Jr. (ed.) (2008) 'Cognitive Dissonance', in *International Encyclopedia of the Social Sciences*, Detroit, Macmillan Reference USA, pp. 599–601. [online] Available from: https://goo.gl/ZuJ1mA (Accessed 29 March 2018)

32   Plato, 427? BCE-347? BCE (1999) *Theaetetus*, [online] Available from: https://www.gutenberg.org/ebooks/1726 (Accessed 29 March 2018)

33   Hiebert, Murray and Klatt, Bruce (eds.) (2001) 'Inclusion, Control, and Affection: Developing Commitment and Teamwork', in *The Encyclopedia of Leadership: A Practical Guide to Popular Leadership Theories and Techniques*, New York, McGraw-Hill Professional, pp. 308–310. [online] Available from: https://goo.gl/QeStgD (Accessed 29 March 2018)

34   Taylor, Rodney L. (ed.) (2005) 'Chien-ai', in *The Illustrated Encyclopedia of Confucianism*, New York, Rosen Publishing, pp. 68–69. [online] Available from: https://goo.gl/BRJGT3 (Accessed 29 March 2018)

35   Barker, Dan (2008) *Godless: How an Evangelical Preacher Became One of America's Leading Atheists*, Berkeley, Calif., Ulysses Press.

36   Benton, Richard P. (1994) 'Xunzi', in Roth, J. K. (ed.), *Ethics, Rev. ed.*, Pasadena, CA, Salem Press, p. 1610. [online] Available from: https://goo.gl/6yqdcp (Accessed 29 March 2018)

37   Jobst, Andrea, Sabass, Lena, Palagyi, Anja, Bauriedl-Schmidt, Christine, et al. (2015)

'Effects of social exclusion on emotions and oxytocin and cortisol levels in patients with chronic depression'. *Journal of Psychiatric Research*, 60, pp. 170–177.

38 Anon (2012) *Jerry DeWitt discusses religion in Little Rock at Arkansas Society of Freethinkers Meeting*, [online] Available from: https://youtu.be/ADNUNai9rF8 (Accessed 29 March 2018)

39 Anon (2013) *Jerry DeWitt & Dan Barker at Ethical Humanist Society, Skokie, IL - 5/11/2013*, [online] Available from: https://youtu.be/m4YZ58eKiaw (Accessed 29 March 2018)

40 Boghossian, Peter G (2013) *A Manual for Creating Atheists*,

41 Anon (n.d.) 'Recovering From Religion'. *Recovering From Religion.* [online] Available from: https://www.recoveringfromreligion.org/ (Accessed 29 March 2018)

42 Anon (n.d.) 'Recovering From Religion - Secular Therapy Project'. [online] Available from: https://www.seculartherapy.org/ (Accessed 31 March 2018)

43 Anon (n.d.) 'Vestigial Tale, Part 1: What science tells us about the human drive to tell

stories'. *CBC Radio.* [online] Available from: https://goo.gl/j96VMJ (Accessed 13 November 2017)

44 Anon (n.d.) 'Vestigial Tale, Part 2: The evolutionary origins of human storytelling'. *CBC Radio.* [online] Available from: https://goo.gl/J5mrLX (Accessed 13 November 2017)

45 McRaney, David (2012) *You Are Not So Smart: Why You Have Too Many Friends on Facebook, Why Your Memory Is Mostly Fiction, and 46 Other Ways You're Deluding Yourself* Reprint edition., New York, Gotham.

46 Carrier, Richard (2012) *Proving history: Bayes's theorem and the quest for the historical Jesus,* Amherst, N.Y., Prometheus Books.

47 McRaney, David (2014) *You Are Now Less Dumb: How to Conquer Mob Mentality, How to Buy Happiness, and All the Other Ways to Outsmart Yourself* Reprint edition., New York, Gotham.

48 Anon (2014) 'deserve | Definition of deserve in US English by Oxford Dictionaries'. *Oxford Dictionaries | English.* [online] Available from: https://en.oxforddictionaries.com/definition/us/deserve (Accessed 29 March 2018)

49 Anon (2003) 'The Architect (A Character in The Matrix)'. *IMDb.* [online] Available from: https://goo.gl/Ppe2pB (Accessed 29 March 2018)

50 Anon (n.d.) 'Kaling Wald lived with husband's corpse, believed he would be resurrected'. [online] Available from: https://goo.gl/EY44bH (Accessed 29 March 2018)

51 Nuwer, Rachel (2014) 'BBC - Future - Will religion ever disappear?' [online] Available from: https://goo.gl/HfPtiI (Accessed 20 December 2014)

52 Grayling, A. C. (2013) *Good Book, The* Reprint edition., New York, Bloomsbury US.

53 Weir, Peter (1998) *The Truman Show*, Drama

54 Wachowski, Andy and Wachowski, Lana (1999) *The Matrix*, Action, Sci-Fi

55 Anon (2016) 'Memory Hackers — NOVA | PBS'. [online] Available from: http://www.pbs.org/wgbh/nova/body/memory-hackers.html (Accessed 31 March 2018)

56 Soeter, Marieke and Kindt, Merel (2015) 'An Abrupt Transformation of Phobic Behavior After a Post-Retrieval Amnesic Agent'. *Biological Psychiatry*, 78(12), pp. 880–886.

57   Friedman, Richard A. (2016) 'Opinion | A Drug to Cure Fear'. *The New York Times*, 22nd January. [online] Available from: https://goo.gl/r2L6iR (Accessed 13 August 2017)

58   Thome, Janine, Koppe, Georgia, Hauschild, Sophie, Liebke, Lisa, et al. (2016) 'Modification of Fear Memory by Pharmacological and Behavioural Interventions during Reconsolidation'. *PLoS ONE*, 11(8), pp. 1–20.

59   Tom Staveley (2016) *Psychology- Merel Kindt's Studies*, [online] Available from: https://youtu.be/HDXWBHCusqs (Accessed 31 March 2018)

60   Messerly, John G. (n.d.) 'Religion's smart-people problem: The shaky intellectual foundations of absolute faith'. [online] Available from: https://goo.gl/lzZfvO (Accessed 29 March 2018)

61   Carol Tavris and Elliot Aronson (2008) *Mistakes Were Made (but Not by Me): Why We Justify Foolish Beliefs, Bad Decisions, and Hurtful Acts*, Harcourt Inc.

62   Newberg, Andrew and Waldman, Mark Robert (2007) *Born to Believe: God, Science, and the Origin of Ordinary and Extraordinary Beliefs* 1st ed., Free Press.

63 Scott-Kakures, Dion (2006) 'Self-Deception', in Borchert, D. M. (ed.), *Encyclopedia of Philosophy*, Detroit, Macmillan Reference USA, pp. 711–717. [online] Available from: https://goo.gl/llNRKn (Accessed 29 March 2018)

64 Fry, Stephen (2008) *Stephen Fry and the Gutenberg printing press*, London, BBC.

65 Davidson, Donald (2004) *Problems of Rationality*, Oxford University Press. [online] Available from: https://goo.gl/gsBrP5 (Accessed 29 March 2018)

66 Martin, Mike W. (1999) 'Self-Deception', in Audi, R. (ed.), *Cambridge Dictionary of Philosophy*, Cambridge, UK, Cambridge University Press, p. 825. [online] Available from: https://goo.gl/6JgvIV (Accessed 29 March 2018)

67 Hirstein, William (2004) *Brain Fiction: Self-Deception and the Riddle of Confabulation*, The MIT Press.

68 Anon (2017) 'A UK Woman Has an Extra Cone Cell in Her Eyes and Can See More Colors'. *Futurism*. [online] Available from: https://goo.gl/Kcz81N (Accessed 16 August 2017)

69 Roberts, Stephen F (2018) 'History of The Quote'. [online] Available from: https://goo.gl/VY1Axs (Accessed 19 February 2018)

70 Big Think (n.d.) *Richard Dawkins: 2 Flaws Plague Unscientific Belief, from Trump & Alt-Right to Religious Doctrine*, [online] Available from: https://youtu.be/n3MmXmAACUM (Accessed 29 March 2018)

71 Anon (2018) 'Genocide of Yazidis by ISIL'. *Wikipedia.* [online] Available from: https://goo.gl/e7fdWy (Accessed 18 February 2018)

72 Kiekeben, Franz (n.d.) 'Broad vs. Narrow Atheism'. *franz kiekeben.* [online] Available from: https://goo.gl/d9SrDZ (Accessed 18 February 2018)

73 Muehlhauser, Luke (n.d.) '17 Kinds of Atheism'. [online] Available from: https://goo.gl/CxjYX6 (Accessed 18 February 2018)

74 Bright, Eric (2017) 'Is it possible to prove a negative?' *BlogSophy.* [online] Available from: https://goo.gl/aQcFd5 (Accessed 25 March 2018)

75 Weinberg, Steven (1999) 'A Designer Universe?' [online] Available from: https://goo.gl/dwMUf2

76 Anon (n.d.) 'Pigeon chess - RationalWiki'. [online] Available from: https://rationalwiki.org/wiki/Pigeon_chess (Accessed 26 March 2018)

77 Clark, Theo (n.d.) 'Moving the Goalposts'. [online] Available from: http://www.skepticsfieldguide.net/2012/04/moving-goalposts.html (Accessed 29 March 2018)

78 Anon (n.d.) 'Moving the goalposts - RationalWiki'. [online] Available from: https://rationalwiki.org/wiki/Moving_the_goalposts (Accessed 29 March 2018)

79 Anon (2017) 'Moving the goalposts'. *Wikipedia.* [online] Available from: https://en.wikipedia.org/wiki/Moving_the_goalposts (Accessed 29 March 2018)

80 Anon (2017) 'Recovering from Religion'. *Wikipedia.* [online] Available from: https://en.wikipedia.org/wiki/Recovering_from_Religion (Accessed 29 March 2018)

81 Anon (n.d.) 'Gish Gallop - RationalWiki'. [online] Available from: https://rationalwiki.org/wiki/Gish_Gallop (Accessed 29 March 2018)

82 Anon (2017) 'Charlatan'. *Wikipedia.* [online] Available from: https://en.wikipedia.org/wiki/Charlatan (Accessed 29 March 2018)

83 Anon (n.d.) 'Bullshit - RationalWiki'. [online] Available from: https://rationalwiki.org/wiki/Bullshit (Accessed 26 March 2018)

84 Anon (n.d.) 'PIDOOMA - RationalWiki'. [online] Available from: https://rationalwiki.org/wiki/PIDOOMA (Accessed 26 March 2018)

85 Bergstrom, Carl T. and West, Jevin (2017) 'Calling Bullshit'. [online] Available from: http://callingbullshit.org/ (Accessed 26 March 2018)

86 Dawkins, Richard (2011) 'Why I refuse to debate with William Lane Craig'. *The Guardian.* [online] Available from: https://goo.gl/9Wa1Cr (Accessed 3 July 2017)

87 Anon (n.d.) 'On the spot fallacy - RationalWiki'. [online] Available from: https://rationalwiki.org/wiki/On_the_spot_fallacy (Accessed 29 March 2018)

88 Berne, Eric (1996) *Games People Play: The Basic Handbook of Transactional Analysis.*, New York, Ballantine Books.

89 University of Notre Dame (2011) *The God Debate II: Harris vs. Craig*, [online] Available from: https://youtu.be/yqaHXKLRKzg (Accessed 29 March 2018)

90 Durant, Will (1961) *The story of philosophy: the lives and opinions of the greater philosophers*, New York, Washington Square Press.

[Blank page]

[Blank page]

www.ingramcontent.com/pod-product-compliance
Lightning Source LLC
Chambersburg PA
CBHW060512090426
42735CB00011B/2190